Left Behind

An Alaska Legend
of Betrayal, Courage
and Survival

THE EXCHANGE

How do
challenges bring
out the best and
worst in people?

Left Behind

An Alaska
Legend of Betrayal, Courage
and Survival

By VELMA WALLIS
Illustrations by Jim Grant

 HAMPTON-BROWN

Hampton-Brown
P.O. Box 223220
Carmel, California 93922
800-333-3510
www.hampton-brown.com

Printed in the United States of America

ISBN-13: 978-0-7362-3163-3
ISBN-10: 0-7362-3163-3

07 08 09 10 11 12 13 14 15 10 9 8 7 6 5 4 3 2

Table of Contents

INTRODUCTION

In *Left Behind*, author Velma Wallis tells the story of two Athabascan Native American women who struggle to **survive** in the Alaskan wilderness. Wallis first learned of this story from her mother, when she was a young girl. Storytelling forms an important tradition in Athabascan culture. Athabascan Indians often tell **legends** to teach important lessons to their children.

Athabascans have lived in Alaska for centuries. In the past, Athabascans lived as nomads, or people who often moved their homes from place to place in search of food. By 1900, the Athabascan people started to live permanently in villages or camps. Although the Athabascan lifestyle has changed, there is still a strong effort to keep the Athabascan culture and languages alive. Athabascans also continue to have respect for the environment.

Wallis's characters are members of the Gwich'in band, or group. In the past, Athabascan groups, like the Gwich'in, usually had twenty to forty members. All of

Key Concepts

survive *v.* to stay alive in a difficult situation

legend *n.* story told from one generation to the next

the members moved from camp to camp in search of food. The Gwich'in once lived and hunted along the Yukon and Porcupine rivers. Each group of Athabascans had their own territories for camping, hunting, and fishing. If one group went into another's territory, it often led to violent battles.

The biggest challenge for these groups was to survive the Alaskan weather. Temperatures in Alaska can be extreme, going from below freezing in the winter to more than 100 degrees in the summer.

Alaska, the Setting for *Left Behind*

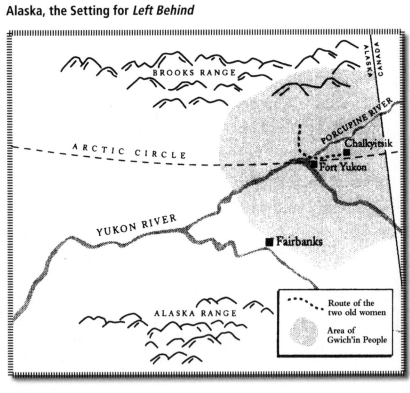

During the warmer seasons, Athabascans spent most of their time searching for food. They often fished for salmon, hunted animals, and gathered plants. In the cold winter, however, Athabascans were often unable to hunt and fish. They usually settled in woods that were near a river, where it was slightly warmer. During these times the Athabascans ate whatever food they saved from the warmer seasons. Each Athabascan had to perform several jobs in order to help the group survive.

Even when each member helped in some way, survival was still difficult. Athabascans often faced starvation. Group members had to be **courageous**. They had to stay together and keep searching for food. Sometimes the struggle was too great, and the group left behind older and weaker members who slowed them down. As their friends and family moved on, these weaker Athabascans died in the wilderness alone.

Left Behind is the legend of two such outcasts, Ch'idzigyaak (CHID-zig-yak) and Sa' (SAH). They are **elder** Athabascan women who are **abandoned** because they are seen as a burden to the group. Now they must survive on their own. Even though the women are very old, they refuse to quit. They agree that if they must die, they should "die trying." The novel tells the story of their heroic battle against starvation and death and their fight to stay strong in the face of great challenges.

Key Concepts

courageous *adj.* showing bravery

elder *adj.* old or oldest member of a group

abandon *v.* to leave a person or object behind in a negative way

From the Author

Each day after cutting wood we would sit and talk in our small tent on the bank at the mouth of the Porcupine River, near where it flows into the Yukon. We would always end with Mom telling me a story. (There I was, long past my youth, and my mother still told me bedtime stories!) One night it was a story I heard for the first time —a story about two old women and their journey through hardship.

What brought the story to mind was a conversation we had earlier while working side by side collecting wood for the winter. Now we sat on our bedrolls and marveled at how Mom in her early fifties still was able to do this kind of hard work while most people of her generation long since had resigned themselves to old age and all of its limitations. I told her I wanted to be like her when I became an elder.

We began to remember how it once was. My grandmother and all those other elders from the past kept themselves busy until they could no longer move or until they died. Mom felt proud that she was able to overcome some of the obstacles of old age and still could get her own winter wood despite the fact that physically, the work was difficult and sometimes agonizing. During our pondering and reflections, Mom remembered this particular story because it was appropriate to all that we thought and felt at that moment.

Later, at our winter cabin, I wrote the story down. I was impressed with it because it not only taught me a lesson that I could use in my life, but also because it was a story about my people and my past—something about me that I could grasp and call mine. Stories are gifts given by an elder to a younger person. Unfortunately, this gift is not given, nor received, as often today because many of our youth are occupied by television and the fast pace of modern-day living. Maybe tomorrow a few of today's generation who were sensitive enough to have listened to their elders' wisdom will have the traditional word-of-mouth stories living within their memory. Perhaps tomorrow's generation also will yearn for stories such as this so that they may better understand their past, their people and, hopefully, themselves.

Sometimes, too, stories told about one culture by someone from another way of life are misinterpreted. This is tragic. Once set down on paper, some stories are readily accepted as history, yet they may not be truthful.

This story of the two old women is from a time long before the arrival of the Western culture, and has been handed down from generation to generation, from person to person, to my mother, and then to me. Although I am writing it, using a little of my own creative imagination, this is, in fact, the story I was told and the point of the story remains the way Mom meant for me to hear it.

This story told me that there is no limit to one's ability—certainly not age—to accomplish in life what one must. Within each individual on this large and complicated world there lives an astounding potential of greatness. Yet it is rare that these hidden gifts are brought to life unless by the chance of fate.

CHAPTER 1
Hunger and cold take their toll

The air stretched tight, quiet and cold over the **vast** land. Tall spruce branches **hung heavily laden with snow, awaiting distant spring winds**. The frosted willows seemed to tremble in the freezing temperatures.

Far off in this seemingly **dismal land were bands** of people dressed in furs and animal skins, huddled close to small campfires. Their weather-burnt faces were stricken with looks of hopelessness as they faced starvation, and the future held little promise of better days.

These nomads were The People of the arctic region of

....

vast wide

hung heavily laden with snow, awaiting distant spring winds
had a lot of snow, which would blow away when spring came

dismal land were bands sad place were groups

Alaska, always on the move in search of food. Where the caribou and other migrating animals roamed, The People followed. But the deep cold of winter **presented special problems**. The moose, their favorite source of food, took refuge from the penetrating cold by staying in one place, and were difficult to find. Smaller, more accessible animals such as rabbits and tree squirrels could not sustain a large band such as this one. And during the cold spells, even the smaller animals either disappeared in hiding or were **thinned by predators, man and animal alike**. So during this unusually bitter chill in the late fall, the land seemed **void of life** as the cold hovered menacingly.

During the cold, hunting required more energy than at other times. Thus, the hunters were fed first, as it was their skills on which The People depended. Yet, with so many to feed, what food they had was depleted quickly. Despite their best efforts, many of the women and children suffered from malnutrition, and some would die of starvation.

In this particular band were two old women cared for by The People for many years. The older woman's name was Ch'idzigyaak, for she reminded her parents of a chickadee bird when she was born. The other woman's name was Sa', meaning "star," because at the time of her birth her mother had been looking at the fall night sky, concentrating on the distant stars to take her mind away from the painful labor contractions.

....

presented special problems made it harder to find food

thinned by predators, man and animals alike eaten by men and other animals

void of life to be without food

The chief would instruct the younger men to set up shelters for these two old women each time the band arrived at a new campsite, and to provide them with wood and water. The younger women pulled the two elder women's possessions from one camp to the next and, in turn, the old women tanned animal skins for those who helped them. The arrangement worked well.

However, the two old women shared a **character flaw** unusual for people of those times. Constantly they complained of aches and pains, and they carried walking sticks to attest to their handicaps. Surprisingly, the others seemed not to mind, despite having been taught from the days of their childhood that weakness was not tolerated among the inhabitants of this harsh motherland. Yet, no one **reprimanded** the two women, and they continued to travel with the stronger ones—until one **fateful** day.

On that day, something more than the cold **hung in the air** as The People gathered around their few flickering fires and listened to the chief. He was a man who stood almost a head taller than the other men. From within the folds of his parka ruff he spoke about the cold, hard days they were to expect and of what each would have to contribute if they were to survive the winter.

Then, in a loud, clear voice he made a sudden announcement: "The council and I have arrived at a decision." The chief paused as if to find the strength to

....

character flaw bad habit
reprimanded scolded, punished
fateful important
hung in the air worried the group

voice his next words. "We are going to have to leave the old ones behind."

His eyes quickly scanned the crowd for reactions. But the hunger and cold **had taken their toll**, and The People did not seem to be shocked. Many expected this to happen, and some thought it for the best. In those days, leaving the old behind in times of starvation was not an unknown act, although in this band it was happening for the first time. **The starkness of the primitive land seemed to demand it**, as the people, to survive, were forced to imitate some of the ways of the animals. Like the younger, more able wolves who shun the old leader of the pack, these people would leave the old behind so that they could move faster without the extra burden.

The older woman, Ch'idzigyaak, had a daughter and a grandson among the group. The chief looked into the crowd for them and saw that they, too, had shown no reaction. Greatly relieved that the unpleasant announcement had been made without incident, the chief instructed everyone to pack immediately. Meanwhile, this brave man who was their leader could not bring himself to look at the two old women, for he did not feel so strong now.

The chief understood why The People who cared for the old women did not **raise objections**. In these hard times, many of the men became frustrated and were angered easily, and one wrong thing said or done could

....

had taken their toll made the people tired and weak

The starkness of the primitive land seemed to demand it Their desperate situation made it seem necessary

raise objections fight the decision

cause an **uproar** and make matters worse. So it was that the weak and beaten members of the tribe kept what dismay they felt to themselves, for they knew that the cold could bring on a wave of panic followed by cruelty and brutality among people fighting for survival.

In the many years the women had been with the band, the chief had come to feel affection for them. Now, he wanted to be away as quickly as possible so that the two old women could not look at him and make him feel worse than he had ever felt in his life.

The two women sat old and small before the campfire with their chins held up proudly, disguising their shock. In their younger days they had seen very old people left behind, but they never expected such a fate. They stared ahead numbly as if they had not heard the chief condemn them to a certain death—to be left alone to fend for themselves in a land that understood only strength. Two weak old women **stood no chance against such a rule**. The news left them without words or action and no way to defend themselves.

Of the two, Ch'idzigyaak was the only one with a family—a daughter, Ozhii Nelii, and a grandson, Shruh Zhuu. She waited for her daughter to protest, but none came, and a deeper sense of shock overcame her. Not even her own daughter would try to protect her. Next to her, Sa' also was stunned. **Her mind reeled** and, though she

....

uproar angry response

stood no chance against such a rule could never survive on their own

Her mind reeled The situation scared her

wanted to cry out, no words came. She felt as if she were in a terrible nightmare where she could neither move nor speak.

As the band slowly trudged away, Ch'idzigyaak's daughter went over to her mother, carrying a bundle of babiche—thickly-stripped raw moosehide that served many purposes. She hung her head in shame and grief, for her mother refused to acknowledge her presence. Instead, Ch'idzigyaak stared unflinchingly ahead.

Ozhii Nelii was in deep turmoil. She feared that, if she defended her mother, The People would settle the matter by leaving her behind and her son, too. Worse yet, **in their famished state**, they might do something even more terrible. She could not chance it.

With those frightening thoughts, Ozhii Nelii silently begged with sorrowful eyes for forgiveness and understanding as she gently laid the babiche down in front of her rigid parent. Then she slowly turned and walked away with a **heaviness in her heart**, knowing she had just lost her mother.

The grandson, Shruh Zhuu, was deeply disturbed by the cruelty. He was an unusual boy. While the other boys competed for their manhood by hunting and wrestling, this one was content to help provide for his mother and the two old women. His behavior seemed to be **outside of the structure of the band's organization handed down from generation to generation**. In this case, the

....

in their famished state as hungry as everyone was

heaviness in her heart great sadness

outside of the structure of the band's organization handed down from generation to generation different from the way boys were supposed to act

women did most of the burdensome tasks such as pulling the well-packed **toboggans**. In addition, much other time-consuming work was expected to be done by the women while the men concentrated on hunting so that the band could survive. No one complained, for that was the way things were and always had been.

Shruh Zhuu held much respect for the women. He saw how they were treated and he disapproved. And while it was explained to him over and over, he never understood why the men did not help the women. But his training told him that he never was to question the ways of The People, for that would be disrespectful. When he was younger, Shruh Zhuu was not afraid to **voice his opinions on this subject, for youth and innocence were his guardians**. Later, he learned that such behavior invited punishment. He felt the pain of the silent treatment when even his mother refused to speak to him for days. So Shruh Zhuu learned that it caused less pain to think about certain things than to speak out about them.

Although he thought abandoning the helpless old women was the worst thing The People could do, Shruh Zhuu was struggling with himself. His mother saw the turmoil raging in his eyes and she knew that he was close to protesting. She went to him quickly and whispered urgently into his ear not to think of it, for the men were desperate enough to commit any kind of cruel action.

....

toboggans sleds

voice his opinions on this subject, for youth and innocence were his guardians say what he thought because he was too young to be punished

Shruh Zhuu saw the men's dark faces and knew this to be true, so he **held his tongue even as his heart continued to rage rebelliously**.

In those days, each young boy was trained to care for his weapons, sometimes better than he cared for his loved ones, for the weapons **were to be his livelihood** when he became a man. When a boy was caught handling his weapon the wrong way or for the wrong purpose, **it resulted in harsh punishment**. As he grew older, the boy would learn the power of his weapon and how much significance it had, not only for his own survival but also for that of his people.

Shruh Zhuu threw all this training and thoughts of his

....

held his tongue even as his heart continued to rage rebelliously did not speak although he felt they were wrong

were to be his livelihood would keep him alive

it resulted in harsh punishment he got in trouble

own safety to the winds. He took from his belt **a hatchet** made of sharpened animal bones bound tightly together with hardened babiche and **stealthily** placed it high in the thick **boughs** of a bushy young spruce tree, well concealed from the eyes of The People.

As Shruh Zhuu's mother packed their things, he turned toward his grandmother. Though she seemed to look right through him, Shruh Zhuu made sure no one was watching as he pointed to his empty belt, then toward the spruce tree. Once more he gave his grandmother a look of hopelessness, and reluctantly turned and walked away to join the others, wishing **with a sinking feeling** that he could do something miraculous to end this nightmarish day.

The large band of famished people slowly moved away, leaving the two women sitting in the same stunned position on their piled spruce boughs. Their small fire cast a soft orange glow onto their weathered faces. A long time passed before the cold brought Ch'idzigyaak out of her stupor. She was aware of her daughter's helpless gesture but believed that her only child should have defended her even in the face of danger. The old woman's heart softened as she thought of her grandson. How could she bear hard feelings toward one so young and gentle? The others made her angry, especially her daughter! Had she not trained her to be strong? Hot, unbidden tears ran from her eyes.

At that moment, Sa' lifted her head in time to see her

....

a hatchet an ax
stealthily quickly and quietly
boughs branches
with a sinking feeling unhappily, sadly

friend's tears. A rush of anger surged within her. How dare they! Her cheeks burned with the humiliation. She and the other old woman were not close to dying! Had they not sewed and tanned for what the people gave them? They did not have to be carried from camp to camp. They were neither helpless nor hopeless. Yet they had been condemned to die.

Her friend had seen eighty summers, she, seventy-five. The old ones she had seen left behind when she was young were so close to death that some were blind and could not walk. Now here she was, still able to walk, to see, to talk, yet . . . bah! Younger people these days looked for easier ways out of hard times. As the cold air smothered the campfire, Sa' came alive with a greater fire within her, **almost as if her spirit had absorbed the energy from the now-glowing embers of the campfire**. She went to the tree and retrieved the hatchet, smiling softly as she thought of her friend's grandson. She sighed as she walked toward her companion, who had not stirred.

Sa' looked up at the blue sky. **To an experienced eye**, the blue this time of winter meant cold. Soon it would be colder yet as night approached. With a worried frown on her face, Sa' kneeled beside her friend and spoke in a gentle but firm voice. "My friend," she said and paused, hoping for more strength than she felt. "We can sit here and wait to die. We will not have long to wait . . .

....

almost as if her spirit had absorbed the energy from the now-glowing embers of the campfire like she was as strong and powerful as their growing fire

To an experienced eye To someone who understood the weather

"Our time **of leaving this world** should not come for a long time yet," she added quickly when her friend looked up with panic-stricken eyes. "But we will die if we just sit here and wait. This would prove them right about our helplessness."

Ch'idzigyaak listened with despair. Knowing that her friend was dangerously close to **accepting a fate of death from cold and hunger**, Sa' spoke more urgently. "Yes, in their own way they have condemned us to die! They think that we are too old and useless. They forget that we, too, have earned the right to live! So I say if we are going to die, my friend, let us die **trying, not sitting**."

....

of leaving this world to die

accepting a fate of death from cold and hunger giving up hope

trying, not sitting as we fight to survive, rather than giving up

BEFORE YOU MOVE ON...

1. Character's Motive Reread pages 20–23. Why does Shruh Zhuu leave his hatchet for his grandmother?

2. Comparisons Reread pages 23–25. How do Ch'idzigyaak and Sa' react differently to their fate?

LOOK AHEAD Read pages 26–34 to see if the women can catch their own food.

CHAPTER 2
"Let us die trying"

Ch'idzigyaak sat quietly as if trying to **make up her confused mind**. *A small feeling of hope sparked in the blackness of her being* as she listened to her friend's strong words. She felt the cold stinging her cheeks where her tears had fallen, and she listened to the silence that The People left behind. She knew that what her friend said was true, that within this calm, cold land waited a certain death if they did nothing for themselves. Finally, **more in desperation than in determination** she echoed her friend's words, "Let us die trying." With that, her friend helped her up off the sodden branches.

....

make up her confused mind decide what to do

A small feeling of hope sparked in the blackness of her being She began to feel a little hopeful

more in desperation than in determination because it was the only thing to do

The women gathered sticks to build the fire and they added pieces of fungus that grew large and dry on fallen cottonwood trees to keep it smoldering. They went around to other campfires to salvage what embers they could find. As they packed to travel, the migrating bands in these times preserved hot coals in hardened mooseskin sacks or birchbark containers filled with ash in which the **embers pulsated**, ready to spark the next campfire.

As night approached, the women cut thin strips from the bundle of babiche, fashioning them into **nooses** the size of a rabbit's head. Then, despite their weariness, the women managed to make some rabbit **snares**, which they immediately set out.

The moon hung big and orange on the horizon as they trudged through the knee-deep snow, searching in the dimness for signs of rabbit life. It was hard to see, and what rabbits existed stayed quiet in the cold weather. But they found several old, hardened rabbit trails frozen solid beneath the trees and arching willows. Ch'idzigyaak tied a babiche noose to a long, thick willow branch and placed it across one of the trails. She made little fences of willows and spruce boughs on each side of the noose to guide the rabbit through the snare. The two women set a few more snares but felt little hope that even one rabbit would be caught.

On their way back to the camp, Sa' heard something **skitter lightly** along the bark of a tree. She stood very still,

....

embers pulsated pieces of wood from the dying fire glowed
nooses circles, loops
snares traps
skitter lightly climb quickly

motioning her friend to do the same. Both women strained to hear the sound once more in the silence of the night. On a tree not far from them, silhouetted in the now-silvery moonlight, they saw an adventurous tree squirrel. Sa' slowly reached to her belt for the hatchet. With her eyes on the squirrel and her movements deliberately slow, she aimed the hatchet toward this **target that represented survival**. The animal's small head came up instantly and as Sa' moved her hand to throw, the squirrel darted up the tree. Sa' **foresaw this**, and, aiming a little higher, ended the small animal's life in one calculating throw with skill and hunting knowledge that she had not used in many seasons.

Ch'idzigyaak let out a deep sigh of relief. The moon's light shone on the younger woman's smiling face as she said

....

target that represented survival squirrel that would save them from starvation

foresaw this knew this would happen

in a proud yet shaky voice, "Many times I have done that, but never did I think I would do it again."

Back at the camp, the women boiled the squirrel meat in snow water and drank the **broth**, saving the small portion of meat to be eaten later, for they knew that otherwise, this could be their last meal.

The two women had not eaten for some time because The People had tried to **conserve** what little food they had. Now they realized why precious food had not been given to them. Why waste food on two who were to die? Trying not to think about what had happened, the two women filled their empty stomachs with the warm squirrel broth and settled down in their tents for the night.

The shelter was made of two large **caribou hides** wrapped around three long sticks shaped into a kind of triangle. Inside were thickly-piled spruce boughs covered with many fur blankets. The women were aware that, although they had been left behind to fend for themselves, The People had done them a good deed by leaving them with all their possessions. They suspected that the chief was responsible for this small kindness. Other less noble members of the band would have decided that the two women soon would die and would have **pilfered** everything except for the warm fur and skin clothing they wore. With these confusing thoughts lingering in their minds, the two frail women dozed.

....

broth soup
conserve save
caribou hides wild-animal skins
pilfered taken

The moonlight shone silently upon the frozen earth as life whispered throughout the land, broken now and then by a lone wolf's melancholy howl. The women's eyes twitched in tired, troubled dreams, and soft, helpless moans escaped from their lips. Then a cry rang out somewhere in the night as the moon **dipped low on the western horizon**. Both women awoke at once, hoping that the awful screech was a part of her nightmare. Again the wail was heard. This time, the women recognized it as the sound of something caught in one of their snares. They were relieved. Fearing that other predators would **beat them to their catch**, the women hurriedly dressed and rushed to their snare sets. There they saw a small, trembling rabbit that lay partially strangled as it eyed them warily. Without hesitation, Sa' went to the rabbit, put one hand around its neck, felt for the beating heart, and squeezed until the small struggling animal went limp. After Sa' reset the snare, they went back to the camp, each feeling **a thread** of new hope.

Morning came, but brought no light to this far northern land. Ch'idzigyaak awoke first. She slowly kindled the fire into a flame as she carefully added more wood. When the fire had died out during the cold night, frost from their warm breathing had accumulated on the walls of caribou skins.

Sighing in dull exasperation, Ch'idzigyaak went outside where **the northern lights** still danced above, and the

....

dipped low on the western horizon began to set in the distance

beat them to their catch find and eat whatever animal they might have caught

a thread the smallest amount

the northern lights colorful lines of light

stars winked in great numbers. Ch'idzigyaak stood for a moment staring up at these wonders. In all her years, the night sky **never failed to fill her with awe**.

Remembering her task, Ch'idzigyaak grabbed the upper rims of the caribou skins, laid them on the ground and briskly brushed off the crystal frost. After putting the skins up again, she went back inside to build up the campfire. Soon moisture dripped from the skin wall, which quickly dried.

Ch'idzigyaak shuddered to think of the melting frost dripping on them in the cold weather. How had they managed before? Ah, yes! The younger ones were always there, piling wood on the fire, peering into the shelter to make sure that their elders' fire did not go out. What a **pampered** pair they had been! How would they survive now?

Ch'idzigyaak sighed deeply, trying not to **dwell** on those dark thoughts, and concentrated instead on tending the fire without waking her sleeping companion. The shelter warmed as the fire crackled, spitting tiny sparks from the dry wood. Slowly, Sa' awoke to this sound and lay on her back for a long time before becoming aware of her friend's movement. Turning her aching neck slowly, she began to smile but stopped as she saw her friend's forlorn look. In a pained grimace, Sa' propped herself up carefully on one elbow and tried to smile encouragingly as she said,

....

never failed to fill her with awe always amazed her
pampered well taken care of; spoiled
dwell focus

"I thought yesterday had only been a dream when I awoke to your warm fire."

Ch'idzigyaak managed a slight smile at the obvious attempt to **lift her spirits** but continued to stare dully into the fire. "I sit and worry," she said after a long silence. "I fear **what lies ahead**. No! Don't say anything!" She held up her hands as her friend opened her mouth to speak.

"I know that you are sure of our survival. You are younger." She could not help but smile bitterly at her remark, for just yesterday they both had been judged too old to live with the young. "It has been a long time since I have been on my own. There has always been someone there to take care of me, and now . . ." She **broke off with a hoarse whisper** as tears fell, much to her shame.

Her friend let her cry. As the tears eased and the older woman wiped her dampened face, she laughed. "Forgive me, my friend. I am older than you. Yet I cry like a baby."

"We are like babies," Sa' responded. The older woman looked up in surprise at such an admission. "We are like helpless babies." A smile twitched her lips as her friend started to look **slightly affronted** by the remark, but before Ch'idzigyaak could take it in the wrong way Sa' went on. "We have learned much during our long lives. Yet there we were in our old age, thinking that we had done our share in life. So we stopped, just like that. No more working like we used to, even though our bodies are still healthy enough to

....

lift her spirits make her feel better
what lies ahead the future and death
broke off with a hoarse whisper stopped talking
slightly affronted a little hurt

do a little more than we expect of ourselves."

Ch'idzigyaak sat listening, **alert to her friend's sudden revelation as to** why the younger ones thought it best to leave them behind. "Two old women. They complain, never satisfied. We talk of no food, and of how good it was **in our days** when it really was no better. We think that we are so old. Now, because we have spent so many years convincing the younger people that we are helpless, they believe that we are no longer of use to this world."

Seeing tears fill her friend's eyes **at the finality of her words**, Sa' continued in a voice heavy with feeling. "We are going to prove them wrong! The People. And death!"

....

alert to her friend's sudden revelation as to aware that her friend now understood

in our days when we were younger

at the finality of her words as Ch'idzigyaak listened to the painful truth she told

She shook her head, motioning into the air. "Yes, it awaits us, this death. Ready to grab us the moment we show **our weak spots**. I fear this kind of death more than any suffering you and I will go through. If we are going to die anyway, let us die trying!"

Ch'idzigyaak stared for a long time at her friend and knew that what she said was true, that death surely would come if they did not try to survive. She was not convinced that the two of them were strong enough to make it through the **harsh season**, but the passion in her friend's voice made her feel a little better. So, instead of feeling sadness because there was nothing further they could say or do, she smiled. "I think we said this before and will probably say it many more times, but yes, let us die trying." And with a sense of strength **filling her like she had not thought possible**, Sa' returned the smile as she got up to prepare for the long day ahead of them.

....

our weak spots any weakness

harsh season winter

filling her like she had not thought possible growing within herself

BEFORE YOU MOVE ON...

1. **Character** Reread pages 27–28. Describe how Sa' catches the squirrel. What does this show about her?

2. **Metaphor** On page 32, Sa' says, "We are like babies." What does she mean?

LOOK AHEAD Where will the women go for safety? Read pages 35–45 to see.

CHAPTER 3
Recalling old skills

That day the women **went back in time to recall** the skills and knowledge that they had been taught from early childhood.

They began by making snowshoes. Usually **birchwood** was collected during late spring and early summer, but today the **young birch would have to do**. They didn't have the correct tools, of course, but the women managed with what they had to split the wood into four parts each, which they boiled in their large birch containers. When the wood became soft, the women bent it roundish and pointed at the tips. Putting two of these

....

went back in time to recall tried to remember

birchwood the wood from the trees

young birch would have to do wood cut before spring would work well enough

half-rounded sides together, the women awkwardly drilled many little holes into both sides with their small, pointed sewing **awls**. The work was hard, but despite their aching fingers the women continued until they finished the task. Earlier, they had soaked the babiche in water. Now they took the softened material, sliced it into thin strips, and wove it onto the snowshoes. **As the babiche hardened with a little help from the campfire**, the women prepared leather bindings for their snowshoes.

When they finished, the women beamed with pride. Then they walked atop the snow with their slightly awkward but serviceable snowshoes to check their rabbit snares and were further cheered to find they had caught another rabbit. The knowledge that a few days before The People had tried to snare rabbits in the area without success made the women feel almost superstitious about their good luck. They went back to the camp feeling lighthearted about all that had been accomplished.

That night the women talked about their plans. They agreed that they could not remain in the fall camp where they had been abandoned, for there were not enough animals on which to survive the long winter. They also were afraid that potential enemies might **come upon** them. Other bands were traveling, too, even in the cold winter, and the women did not want to be exposed to such dangers. They also began to fear their own people because

....

awls tools, needles

As the babiche hardened with a little help from the campfire
As the heat from the fire dried and toughened the strips of rawhide

come upon find and attack

of the broken trust. The two women decided they must move on, fearing that the cold weather would force people to do desperate things to survive, remembering the taboo stories handed down for generations about how some had **turned into cannibals** to survive.

The two women sat in the shelter, thinking about where to go. Suddenly Ch'idzigyaak burst out, "I know of a place!"

"Where?" Sa' asked in an excited voice.

"Do you remember the place where we fished long ago? The creek where the fish were so abundant that we had to build many **caches** to dry them?" The younger woman searched her memory for a moment, and **vaguely the place came to mind**. "Yes, I do remember. But why did we not ever return?" she asked. Ch'idzigyaak shrugged.

....

of the broken trust they could no longer trust them
turned into cannibals eaten other people
caches storage containers
vaguely the place came to mind then she remembered it

She did not know either.

"Maybe The People forgot that place existed," she **ventured**.

Whatever the reason, the two women agreed that it would be a good place to go now and since it was a long distance, they should leave **at once**. The women yearned to be as far away as possible from this place of bad memories.

The following morning they packed. Their caribou skins served many purposes. That day, they served as pulling sleds. Taking the two skins off the tent frame, the women laid the skins flat with the fur facing the snow. They packed their possessions neatly in the skins and laced them tightly shut with long strips of babiche. They fastened long woven ropes of mooseskin leather onto the front of the skin sleds, and each woman tied a rope around her waist. With the fur of the caribou hides sliding lightly across the dry, deep snow and the women's snowshoes making the walking easier, the two women began their long journey.

Temperatures had dropped, and the cold air made the women's eyes sting. **Time and time** again, they had to warm their faces with their bare hands, and they continually wiped tears from their irritated eyes. But their fur and skin clothing served them well, for cold as it was, their bodies remained warm.

The women walked late into the night. They had not gone too far, but both were **bone-weary** and felt as though

....

ventured guessed

at once right away

Time and time Over and over

bone-weary very tired

they had been walking forever. Deciding to **camp**, the women dug deep pits in the snow and filled them with spruce boughs. Then they built a small campfire, boiling the squirrel meat and drinking its broth. They were so tired they soon fell asleep. This time they did not moan or twitch but slept deep and soundlessly.

Morning arrived, and the women awoke to the deep cold surrounding them while the sky above seemed like a bowl of stars. But as the women tried to climb out of their pits, their bodies would not move. Looking into each other's eyes, the women realized they had **pushed their bodies beyond their physical endurance**. Finally, the younger, more determined Sa' managed to move. But the pain was so great that she let out an agonized groan. Knowing this would happen to her, too, Ch'idzigyaak lay still for awhile, gathering courage to withstand the pain she knew would come. Finally, she, too, made her way slowly and painfully out of the snow shelter, and the women limped around the camp to loosen their stiff joints. After they chewed on the remaining squirrel meat, they continued their journey, slowly pulling their laden toboggans.

That day would be remembered as one of the longest and hardest of the days to come. They stumbled numbly on, many times falling down into the snow from **sheer fatigue** and old age. Yet they pushed on, almost in

....

camp stop and rest
pushed their bodies beyond their physical endurance worked longer and harder than they should have
sheer fatigue complete exhaustion; being so tired

desperation, knowing that each step brought them nearer to their destination.

The distant sunlight that appeared for a short while each day **peeped hazily** through the ice fog that hung in the air. Now and again, blue skies could be seen, but mostly the women noticed only their own frosty breath coming in thick swirls. Freezing their lungs was another worry, and they took care not to work too hard in the cold and, if **such work was unavoidable**, they wore a protective covering over their faces. This could cause **irritating side effects**, such as frost buildup where the covering brushed against their faces. However, the women did not notice such minor discomforts compared with their aching limbs, stiff joints, and swollen feet. Sometimes even the heavy sleds seemed to serve a purpose by keeping the women from falling flat on their faces as they pulled onward with the ropes wrapped around their chests.

....

desperation fear
peeped hazily could not be seen well
such work was unavoidable they had no choice
irritating side effects problems that bothered them

As the few hours of daylight slipped away, the women's
eyes readjusted to the darkness that began to enfold them.
But they knew that night had not yet arrived and that there
was still time to move. When it became time to camp, the
women found themselves on a large lake. They could see
the outline of trees along the shore and they knew that the
forest would be a better place to camp. But they were so
exhausted they could go no farther. Again they dug a deep
pit in the snow, and after **snuggling down** and covering
themselves with their skin blankets they were soon asleep.
The thick skin and fur clothing held their body heat and
protected them from the cold air. The snow pit was as
warm as any shelter aboveground, so the women slept,
mindless of freezing temperatures that made even the
most ferocious northern animals seek shelter.

The next morning, Sa' awoke first. The long sleep and
cold air cleared her mind considerably. With a **twisting
grimace** she stuck her head out of the hole to look around.
She saw the outline of trees on the shore and remembered
how they had been too tired to complete their crossing of
the lake.

She got up slowly, not wanting to **disturb her friend's
slumber** and knowing that with a wrong move her
stiffened body would lock up and refuse to go farther.
A smile hovered around her lips as she thought of how
she and her friend had complained loudly and often of

....

snuggling down moving into the snow pit
mindless unaware
twisting grimace painful expression on her face
disturb her friend's slumber wake her friend

their minor aches and pains a few days before, and of the walking sticks they had used until forgetting them at the camp the day before. Slowly stretching in the chilly air, she **made a mental note** to remind her friend of this when the right time came. They could laugh over the fact that for years they had carried those sticks around to help them walk better and now, somehow, they had managed many miles without them. Putting on her snowshoes, Sa' walked about to loosen the stiffness in her sore joints.

From within the snow pit, Ch'idzigyaak looked up at her **more agile** companion who slowly circled the shelter. Ch'idzigyaak was still tired and feeling miserable. But she knew she must do her best to **stand beside** her friend through this hardship. She had lived long enough to know that if she gave up, her friend would give up, too. So she forced herself to move, but the pain that filled her body made her lie back down, and let out a deep sigh.

Sa' saw that Ch'idzigyaak was having a hard time, so she reached down to help her climb out of the pit. Together they grunted, struggling to move. Soon they were walking again, and kept right on going until they reached the edge of the lake. There, they built a fire and, after eating some of the rabbit meat they had carefully **rationed**, they returned for their sleds and resumed their journey.

The frozen lakes seemed endless. Struggling through the many spruce trees, willow thickets, and thorn patches

....

made a mental note thought
more agile younger and stronger
stand beside keep trying and help
rationed saved and divided into small pieces

that lay between the lakes wore the women out until they felt as if they had traveled many more miles than they had. Despite having to **make many detours around obstacles**, the women never completely lost their sense of direction. Sometimes, **fatigue clouded their judgement**, and they found themselves straying slightly off course or going in circles, but they soon found their way again. In vain, they hoped that the **slough they sought** would appear suddenly. Indeed, there were times when one of them would fantasize that they had reached their destination. But the constant reminders of the intense cold and aching bones brought them quickly back to reality.

On the fourth night, the women almost stumbled onto the slough. Everything around them stood shrouded under silvery moonlight. Shadows stretched beneath the many trees and over the slough. The women stood on the bank for a few moments, resting as their eyes took in the beauty of that special night. Sa' marveled at the power the land held over people like herself, over the animals, and even over the trees. They all depended on the land, and if its rules were not obeyed, quick and unjudgemental death could fall upon the careless and unworthy. Ch'idzigyaak looked at her friend as Sa' sighed deeply. "What's the matter?" she asked.

Sa's face creased in a sad smile. "Nothing is wrong, my friend. We are on the right trail after all. I was thinking

....

make many detours around obstacles change their direction many times for safety

fatigue clouded their judgement their physical weakness made them feel confused

slough they sought creek they were looking for

about how it used to be that the land was easy for me to live on, and now it seems not to want me. Perhaps it is just my aching joints that are making me complain."

Ch'idzigyaak laughed. "Perhaps it is because our bodies are just too old, or maybe we are out of shape. Maybe the time will come when we will **spring across this land** again." Sa' joined in the joke.

Such **musings** were meant only to lift their spirits and the women knew that their journey was not over, nor would their struggle for survival become easier. Although they had grown soft in their old age, Ch'idzigyaak and Sa' knew they would **pay a high price of hard toil before the land yielded them any comforts**.

The two women walked down the winding slough until they came upon a large river. Even in times of cold weather, the swishing undercurrents of the river eroded the ice and made it thin and dangerous to walk on. The women realized this as they carefully inched their way across the quiet river, keeping their senses alert for the sound of cracking ice or any hint of steam rising from between the ice chinks.

....

spring across this land be like young people

musings thoughts

pay a high price of hard toil before the land yielded them any comforts need to work hard to find food and build a shelter

When they finally reached the other side, **the tension and fatigue** left both women mentally and physically **drained**. With what little energy remained, they numbly set to the task of building yet another overnight shelter.

....

the tension and fatigue stress and weakness

drained tired; without energy

BEFORE YOU MOVE ON...

1. **Inference** Reread pages 36–38. The women are tired but they decide to move on. Is this a good idea? Why or why not?

2. **Comparisons** Reread pages 41–42. How have Sa' and Ch'idzigyaak changed since the beginning of the story?

LOOK AHEAD Read pages 46–53 to see if Ch'idzigyaak gives up.

CHAPTER 4
A painful journey

Nights past *when they had managed to build shelters were nothing compared to this one, for the women were so tired they could barely move. In blind determination they stumbled about gathering spruce boughs for their beds and large chunks of wood for the campfire. Finally, they huddled together and stared **as if hypnotized** into the large orange blaze they **ignited** from the live coals carried from the first campsite. Soon they slipped mindlessly off to sleep. They did not hear the lonesome howl of a distant wolf, and before they knew it the cold air of morning **brought them back to their senses**.*

....

Nights past *Previous nights*
as if hypnotized *in a sleepy state*
ignited *lit*
brought them back to their senses *woke them*

They had fallen asleep leaning against one another and somehow managed to stay in that position all night. Because they were sitting up on their legs, the women knew getting up would not be easy. They sat still for a long time. Then Sa' **made an effort to rise**, but her legs had lost their feeling. She grunted and tried again. Meanwhile, Ch'idzigyaak closed her eyes tightly and pretended to be asleep. She did not want to face the day.

Sa' gathered a little courage to force herself to move, but the aches in her bones proved to be too much for her this time. Again they had pushed their bodies beyond their limits. Without meaning to, Sa' let out a painful moan, and she felt a great urge to cry. She hung her head, **defeated by** all they had been through these past few days, and the cold made her feel even more despair. As much as she wanted to, her body would not move. She was too stiff.

Ch'idzigyaak listened **lethargically** to her friend's sniffles. She was amazed that she could sit and listen to Sa' cry and feel no emotion. Perhaps it was not meant for them to go on. Perhaps the young ones were right—she and Sa' were fighting **the inevitable**. It would be easy for them to snuggle deeper into the warmth of their fur clothing and fall asleep. They would not have to prove anything to anyone anymore. Perhaps the sleep that Sa' feared would not be so bad after all. At least, Ch'idzigyaak thought to herself, it would not be as bad as this.

....

made an effort to rise tried to stand
defeated by feeling tired and weak from
lethargically lazily and without much energy
the inevitable against certain death

Yet, for as little will as her older friend had, Sa' possessed enough determination for both of them. Shrugging off the cold, the pain in her sides, her empty stomach, and the numbness in her legs, she struggled to get up and this time succeeded. As had become her morning habit, she limped around the campsite until feeling slowly began to **course through her bloodstream**. When the circulation returned, there was more pain. But Sa' concentrated her attention on gathering more wood to build the fire. Then she boiled a rabbit head to make a tasty broth.

Ch'idzigyaak watched all this from between **narrowed lids**. She did not want her friend to know that she was awake, for then, Ch'idzigyaak felt, she would be obligated to move, and she did not want to move. Not now and not ever. She would stay exactly as she was, and perhaps death would **steal her quickly away from** the suffering. But her body was not ready to give in just yet. Instead of **slipping blissfully into oblivion**, Ch'idzigyaak suddenly felt the urgent need to relieve her bladder. She tried to ignore this, but soon her bladder could wait no more, and with a loud grunt she felt her bladder letting go. In quick panic she jumped up and headed for the willows, startling her friend. When Ch'idzigyaak came out of the willows looking slightly guilty, Sa' tilted her head in wonder. "Is something wrong?" she asked. Ch'idzigyaak, feeling embarrassed, admitted, "I surprised myself by how fast I

....

course through her bloodstream return to her legs
narrowed lids half-closed eyes
steal her quickly away from end
slipping blissfully into oblivion letting death come

moved. I did not think I would be able to move at all!"

Sa' was thinking of the day ahead. "After we have eaten, we should try to move on, even if we go only a little way today," she said. "Each step brings us closer to where we are going. Although I do not feel good today, my mind **has power over** my body, and it wants us to move on instead of staying here to rest—which is what I want to do." Ch'idzigyaak listened as she ate her portion of the rabbit head and broth. She, too, felt like staying there for a while. In fact, she desperately wanted to stay. But after putting aside her foolish thoughts, she felt ashamed and reluctantly agreed they should move on.

Sa' felt a slight disappointment when Ch'idzigyaak agreed to resume their journey, wondering if deep within her she had hoped Ch'idzigyaak would refuse to move. But it was too late **for second thoughts**. So both women tied the ropes around their thin waists and pulled onward. As they walked, they kept their eyes open for signs of animals, for their food was nearly gone, and meat was their **prime source of energy**. Without it, **their struggle would be over soon**. Sometimes, the women stopped to discuss the route they had chosen and to ask themselves if it was the correct way. But the river led in only one direction from the slough, so the women walked along the riverbank as they kept a lookout for the narrow creek that would lead them to a place remembered for its plentiful fish long ago.

....

has power over is stronger than
for second thoughts to change things now
prime source of energy main food source
their struggle would be over soon they would die

The days dragged on as the women slowly pulled their sleds across the deep snow. On the sixth day, Sa', who had grown accustomed to staring **dully** only at the path ahead, happened to glance up. Across the river she saw the opening to the creek. "We are there," she said in a soft, breathless voice. Ch'idzigyaak looked at her friend, then at the creek. "Except we are on the wrong side," she said. Sa' had to smile at her friend, who always seemed to find the negative side of a situation. Too tired to offer a **lighter point of view**, Sa' sighed to herself as she motioned to her friend to follow.

This time the two women did not worry about hidden cracks beneath the ice. They were too tired. Mindless of the danger, they crossed the frozen river and kept right on going up the **tributary**. The women walked until late that night. The moon slowly **emerged** over the trees until it hovered above them, lighting their way along the narrow creek. Although they had walked more hours than they had on earlier days, the women continued on. They felt sure the old campsite was near and they wanted to reach their destination that night.

Just about the time Ch'idzigyaak was ready to beg her friend to stop, she saw the campsite. "Look over there!" she cried. "There are the fishracks we hung so long ago!" Sa' stopped and suddenly felt weak. It was with great effort that she stood on her shaking legs, for a feeling of somehow

....

dully lifelessly
lighter point of view more positive way of thinking
tributary stream
emerged appeared

coming home suddenly overwhelmed her.

Ch'idzigyaak moved closer to her friend and gently placed an arm around her. They looked at each other and felt a **surge** of powerful emotion that left them speechless. They had traveled all this way by themselves. Good memories came back to them about the place where they had shared much happiness with friends and family. Now, because **of an ugly twist of fate**, they were here alone, betrayed by those same people. Because they were **thrown together** in hardship, the two women developed a sense of knowing what the other was thinking, and Sa' was usually the more sensitive one.

"It is better not to think of why we are here," she said. "We must set up our camp here tonight. Tomorrow we will talk." Clearing the bitter emotion from her throat, Ch'idzigyaak heartily agreed. So, with slow, dragging movements, the two women climbed up the low bank of the creek and walked to the campsite, where they found an old tent frame that they used for shelter that night.

Though their clothing **shielded** them from the awful cold, the caribou skins did a better job. Coals from the fire pulsated amidst the ash all through the night and kept the shelter warm. Finally, the morning cold seeped through, and the women began to stir. Sa' was the first to move. This time her body did not protest so much as she moved about the shelter, placing the wood they had gathered

....

surge sudden amount
of an ugly twist of fate the band left them
thrown together forced to stay together
shielded protected

the night before on the tiny embers still burning in the fireplace. After a few moments of softly blowing the dried sticks, a flame began **a gentle dance** as it spread onto the bundle of dry willows. Soon the shelter was warm and glowing.

That day, the women worked steadily, unmindful of their aching joints. They knew they would have to hurry to make final preparations for the worst of the winter, for even colder weather lay ahead. So they spent the day piling snow high around the shelter to **insulate it** and gathering all the loose wood they could find. Then without resting, they set a long line of rabbit snares, for the area **was rich in willow**, and there were many signs of rabbit life. Nighttime had arrived when the women made their way back to the camp. Sa' boiled the **remains of the rabbit's innards** and the women feasted on the last of their food. After that, they leaned against their bedding and stared into the campfire.

---

a gentle dance to grow

insulate it keep the warmth inside the shelter

was rich in willow had many willow trees

remains of the rabbit's innards leftover rabbit

BEFORE YOU MOVE ON...

1. **Cause and Effect** Reread pages 48–49. Ch'idzigyaak wants to give up. Why does she decide to keep going?

2. **Viewing** Look at the illustration on page 52. What can you learn about the camp from this picture?

LOOK AHEAD What were the women's lives like in the past? Read to page 67 to find out.

The two women had not known each other well before being abandoned. They had been two neighbors who **thrived on** each other's bad habit of complaining and on sharing conversations about things that did not matter. Now, their old age and their cruel fate were all they had in common. So it was that night, at the end of their painful journey together, they did not know how to **converse in companionship**, and instead, each woman dwelled on her own thoughts.

Ch'idzigyaak's mind went immediately to her daughter and grandson. She wondered if they were all right. A surge of hurt streaked through her as she thought about her daughter again. It was still hard for Ch'idzigyaak to believe that her own **flesh and blood** would refuse to **come to her aid**. As the self-pity overwhelmed her, Ch'idzigyaak fought the tears that threatened to spill from her eyes, and her lips formed a thin, rigid line. She would not cry! This was the time to be strong and to forget! But with that thought a huge single tear dripped down. She looked at Sa' and saw that she also was lost deep in thought. Ch'idzigyaak was perplexed by her friend. Except for a few moments of weakness, the woman next to her seemed strong and sure of herself, almost as if she were challenged by all of this. Curiosity replaced her pain and Sa' was startled when Ch'idzigyaak spoke.

"Once when I was a little girl, they left my grandmother

....

thrived on increased; added to
converse in companionship talk as friends
flesh and blood family
come to her aid help her

behind. She could no longer walk and could hardly see. We were so hungry that people were **staggering around**, and my mother whispered that she was afraid that people would think of eating people. I had not heard of anything like this before, but my family told stories of some who had grown desperate enough to do such things. My heart filled with fear as I **clung** to my mother's hand. If someone looked into my eyes, I would turn my head quickly, fearing he might take notice of me and consider eating me. That is how much fear I had. I was hungry, too, but somehow it didn't matter. Perhaps it was because I was so young and had my family all around me. When they talked about leaving my grandmother behind, I was **horrified**. I remember my father and brothers arguing with the rest of the men, but when my father came back to the shelter, I looked at his face and knew what would happen. Then I looked at my grandmother. She was blind and too deaf to hear what was going on." Ch'idzigyaak took a deep breath before continuing with her story.

"When they bundled her up and put her blankets all around her, I think Grandmother sensed what was happening because as we began to leave the camp I could hear her crying." The older woman **shuddered** at the memory.

"Later, when I grew up, I learned that my brother and father went back to end my grandmother's life, for they

....

staggering around having trouble walking
clung held on tightly
horrified deeply upset
shuddered shook uncomfortably

did not want her to suffer. And they burned her body in case anyone thought of filling their bellies with her flesh. Somehow, we survived that winter, though my only real memory of that time was that it was not a happy one. I remember other times of empty stomachs, but none as bad as that one winter."

Sa' smiled sadly, understanding her friend's painful memories. She, too, remembered. "When I was young, I was like a boy," she began. "I was always with my brothers. I learned many things from them. Sometimes, my mother would try to make me sit **still** and sew, or learn **that which I would have to know** when I became a woman. But my father and brothers always **rescued me**. They liked me the way I was." She smiled at her memories.

"Our family was different from most. My father and mother let us do almost anything. We did chores like everyone else, but after they were done, we could explore. I never played with other children, only with my brothers. I am afraid I did not know what growing up was about because I was having so much fun. When my mother asked me if I had become a woman yet, I did not understand. I thought she meant in age, **not in that way**. And summer after summer, she would ask me the same question, and each time she looked more worried. I did not pay much attention to her. But as I grew as tall as my mother and just a little shorter than my brothers, people looked at

....

still in one place
that which I would have to know important things for
rescued me let me be myself
not in that way not physically a woman

me in a strange way. Girls younger than me already were **with child and man**. Yet I was still free like a child." Sa' laughed heartily as she now knew why she received all those strange looks from people then.

"I began to hear them laugh at me behind my back and I became confused. In a way, I did not care what people thought about me, so I continued to hunt, fish, explore, and do what I pleased. My mother tried to make me stay home and work, but I **rebelled**. My brothers had taken women, and I told my mother she had plenty of help, and **with that I would escape**. When my mother turned to my father to **discipline** me, I would show up with a huge bundle of ducks, fish, or some other food, and my father would say, 'Leave her alone.' Then I grew older, beyond that age when women should have man and child, and everyone was talking about me. I could not understand why, for although I was not with a man and having children, I was still doing my share of the work by providing food. There were times when I brought more food than the men. This did not seem to please them. About this time in my life, we experienced our worst winter. It was cold like this." Sa' motioned with her hand.

"Even babies died, and grown men began to panic, for as hard as they tried they could not find enough animals to eat. There was an old woman in our group whom I rarely noticed. The chief decided we had to move on in

....

with child and man married and having children
rebelled did not listen to her
with that I would escape then my mother left me alone
discipline punish

our search for food. There was a rumor that far away we would find caribou. This excited everyone.

"The old woman had to be carried. The chief did not want this burden, so he told everyone that we would leave her behind. No one argued, except me. My mother tried to **stifle me**, but I was young and unthinking. She told me that this was to be done for the sake of the whole group. She seemed like a cold, unfeeling stranger as she tried to talk me out of my protest, but I angrily **brushed her off**. I was shocked and furious. I felt that The People were being lazy and were not thinking clearly. It was my job to **talk some sense into them**. And being who I was, I spoke up for the woman whom I hardly knew existed until then. I asked the men if they thought they were no better than the wolves who would **shun** their old and weak.

"The chief was a cruel man. I had avoided him until the day I stood before him and shouted angry words at his face. I could see that he was twice as angry as I was, but I could not stop myself. Even though I knew that the chief disliked me, I argued on, not listening to him as he tried to answer my accusations. His action was wrong, and I meant to make it right. As I continued to talk, I was unaware of the shock that awakened the group from its malnourished lethargy. A fearful look fell upon the chief's face and he put his large hand over my mouth. 'All right, strange young girl,' he said in a loud voice that I knew was meant to

....

stifle me stop me from speaking
brushed her off did not listen to her
talk some sense into them show them their mistake
shun leave

humiliate me. I could feel my chin go up farther so that he could see that I remained proud and unafraid. 'You will stay with the old one,' he said. I could hear my mother gasp, and my own heart sank. Yet I would not yield as I stared unblinkingly into his eyes.

"My family was deeply hurt, but pride and shame kept them from protesting. They did not want a daughter who would take such a stand against the strong leaders of the group. I did not think the leaders were strong. The chief acted as if I did not exist after that, and I was ignored by everyone else except my family, who begged me to apologize to the leader. But I would not **give in**. My pride grew with each moment the others pretended I was not there, and I continued to plead for the old woman's life." Sa' broke into laughter at her **impetuous** youth.

"What happened after that?" Ch'idzigyaak wanted to know.

Sa' paused as she deeply inhaled the pain from those long-ago memories. Continuing in a **subdued** voice, she said, "After they left, I was not so brave. There were no animals to be found for miles around. But I was determined to show what could be done **by my good intentions**. So the old woman—I never did know her name, for I was too busy trying to keep us alive—and I ate mice, owls, and anything else that moved. I killed it, and we ate it. The woman died that winter. Then I was alone.

....

give in say I was sorry
impetuous unthinking, impatient
subdued quiet
by my good intentions since I felt I was right

Not even my pride and usual carefree ways could help me. I talked to myself all the time. Who else was there? They would think I was crazy if The People returned to find me talking to the air. At least you and I have each other," Sa' told her friend, who nodded in **wholehearted** agreement.

"Then I realized the importance of being with a large group. The body needs food, but the mind needs people. When the sun finally came hot and long on the land, I explored the country. One day as I was walking along, talking to myself as usual, someone said, 'Who are you talking to?' For a moment I thought I was hearing things. I stopped **in my tracks** and turned slowly to find a big, strong-looking man with his arms crossed, smiling at me in a bold manner. Many feelings ran through me at that moment. I was surprised, embarrassed, and angry all at once. 'You scared me!' I said, trying to cover up my real feelings. Because my cheeks were **burning**, I knew I did not fool him, for his grin grew deeper. He asked me what I was doing out there alone, and I told him my story. I felt at that moment that I could trust him. He told me that the same thing happened to him. Only he was **banished** because he was foolish enough to fight over a woman who was meant for another man. We were together a long time before we became a man and woman together. I never saw my family again, and it was years later that we joined the band.

"Then he tried to fight with a bear and died. Foolish

....

wholehearted complete
in my tracks suddenly
burning bright red from embarrassment
banished sent to live away from his band

man," she added **with grudging admiration**, as a deep sadness **weighed down** her face.

It was the first time Ch'idzigyaak saw her friend so sad, and she broke the silence by saying, "You were luckier than I, for when it became apparent that I was not interested in taking a man, I was forced to live with a man much older than me. I hardly knew him. It was years before we had our child. He was older than I am now when he died."

Sa' laughed. "The People would have chosen a man for me, too, had I been with them much longer." After a momentary silence, she continued. "Now here we are, truly old. I hear our bones creaking, and we are left behind **to fend for** ourselves." The women fell into silence as they struggled with their emotions. They lay on their warm beds as the cold earth trembled outside. They thought about the experiences they had shared. As they fell into an exhausted sleep, each woman felt more **at home** because of her new knowledge of the other and because each had survived hard times before.

Days shortened as the sun sank deeper under the horizon. It grew so cold there were times when the women jumped as the trees around them cracked loudly from the cold pressure. Even the willows snapped. But as the women settled down they also became depressed. They feared the savage wolves that howled in the distance. Other imagined fears tormented them as well, for there was plenty of time

....

with grudging admiration feeling a little respect
weighed down showed on
to fend for to take care of
at home comfortable

to think as the dark days drifted slowly by. In what daylight they had, the two women forced themselves to move. They spent all their waking hours collecting firewood from underneath the deep snow. Though food was scarce, warmth was their main concern, and at night they would sit and talk, trying to keep each other from the loneliness and fears that threatened to overcome them. The People rarely spent precious time **in idle conversation**. When they did speak, it was to communicate rather than to socialize. But these women made an exception during the long evenings. They talked. And a **sense of mutual respect** developed as each learned of the other's past hardships.

Many days went by before the women caught more rabbits. It had been some time since they had eaten a full meal. They managed to preserve their energy by boiling spruce boughs to serve as a minty tea, but it made the stomach sour. Knowing it was dangerous to eat anything solid after such a diet, the two women first boiled the rabbit meat to make a nourishing broth, which they drank slowly. After a day of drinking the broth, the women cautiously ate one ham off a rabbit. As the days passed, they allowed themselves more portions, and soon their energy was restored.

With wood piled high around the shelter like a **barricade**, the women found that they had more time to **forage** for food. The hunting skills they learned in

....

in idle conversation talking without a clear purpose
sense of mutual respect shared regard
barricade wall
forage search

their youth reemerged, and each day the women would walk farther from the shelter to set their rabbit snares and to **keep an eye out** for any other animals small enough to kill. One of the rules they had been taught was that if you set snares for animals you must check them regularly. Neglecting your snareline brought bad luck. So, despite the cold and their own physical discomforts, the two women checked their snares each day and usually found a rabbit to reward them.

At nightfall, when their daily chores were completed, the women wove the rabbit fur into blankets and clothing, such as mittens and face coverings. Sometimes, to **break the monotony**, one would present a woven rabbit-fur hat or mittens to the other. This always brought wide smiles.

As the days slowly passed, the weather lost its cold edge, and the women **savored moments of glee**—they had survived the winter! They regained what energy they had lost and now they kept busy collecting more firewood, checking the rabbit snares and scouting the vast area for other animals. Though the women had lost the habit of complaining, they grew tired of the daily fare of rabbit meat and found themselves dreaming of other **game** to

....

keep an eye out look
break the monotony keep from being bored
savored moments of glee were much happier
game animals

eat, such as willow grouse, tree squirrels, and beaver meat.

One morning, as Ch'idzigyaak awoke, she felt something was not quite right. Her heart pumped rapidly as she slowly got up, fearing the worst, and peeked out of the shelter. At first, all seemed still. Then suddenly she spotted a **flock of willow grouse pecking at some tree debris** that had fallen not far away. With trembling hands, she quietly got a long, thin strand of babiche out of her sewing bag and slowly crept out of the tent. Selecting a long stick from the nearby woodpile, she fashioned a noose at the end and began to crawl toward the flock.

Nervously, the birds started to cluck as they became aware of the woman's presence. Knowing that the birds were about to **take flight**, Ch'idzigyaak stopped for a few minutes to give them time to calm down. They were not too far from her now, and she hoped that Sa' would not awake and make a noise that would scare away the birds. With knees aching and hands slightly trembling, Ch'idzigyaak slowly pushed the stick forward. Some grouse excitedly flew away to another patch of willows nearby, but she **steadfastly ignored** them as she continued to lift the stick slowly as the remaining birds walked about faster. Ch'idzigyaak concentrated on the grouse closest to her. It made small movements towards the noose, its head nodding back to front. As the birds started noisily to run and fly off, Ch'idzigyaak shoved the noose forward until the

....

flock of willow grouse pecking at some tree debris group of large birds eating pieces from a tree

take flight fly away

steadfastly ignored did not pay any attention to

bird's head slipped right into it. Then she jerked the stick upward as the bird **squawked** and twisted until it hung motionless. Standing up with the dead grouse in her hand, Ch'idzigyaak turned toward the tent to find her friend's face wreathed in smiles. Ch'idzigyaak smiled back.

Looking into the air, Ch'idzigyaak took note of a warmth in the air. "The weather gets better," Sa' said softly and the older woman's eyes widened in surprise. "I should have noticed. Had it been cold, I would have frozen **in my position of a sneaky fox**." The women found great laughter in this as they went back into the shelter to prepare the meat of a different season to come. After that morning, the weather fluctuated between bitter cold and then warm and snowy days. That the women did not catch another bird failed to **dampen their spirits**, for the days gradually grew longer, warmer, and brighter.

....

squawked cried out

in my position of a sneaky fox as I bent over and tried to catch that bird

dampen their spirits sadden them

The routes on this map were taken from a regular map of the Yukon Flats area, with the help of my mother. The winter trails are not historically accurate in detail but do show the general areas through which the Gwich'in people traveled for many years before the coming of the Western culture.

Many winter and summer paths were used by the Gwich'in people but through the years, these trails either have been forgotten or changed by younger generations seeking shortcuts, or by natural events.

N

Tiveh Jan

Nuttr'ihk'it

Dhohts'a

Han Gwachoh (Yukon River)

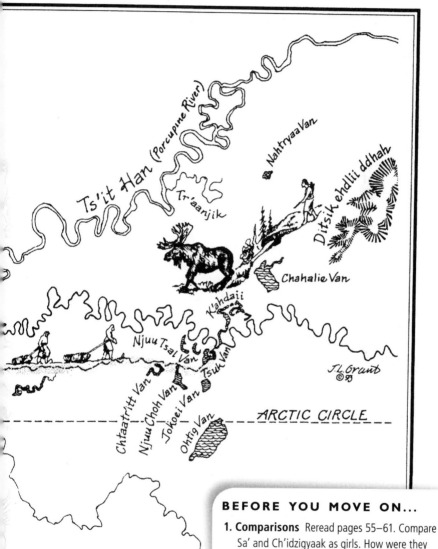

Ts'it Han (Porcupine River)

Nahtryaa Van

Ditsik ehdlii ddhah

Tr'aanjik

Chahalie Van

K'ahdaii

Njuu Tsal Van

Tsuk Van

J.L.Grant ©93

Chtaatritt Van

Njuu Choh Van

Jokoei Van

Ohtig Van

ARCTIC CIRCLE

BEFORE YOU MOVE ON...

1. **Comparisons** Reread pages 55–61. Compare Sa' and Ch'idzigyaak as girls. How were they different?

2. **Mood** Reread pages 63 and 65. How does the mood of the story change after the women survive the winter?

LOOK AHEAD Read pages 68–78 to find out what mistake Ch'idzigyaak and Sa' make.

CHAPTER 5
Saving a cache of fish

*S*oon *winter was gone and the two old women spent more time hunting game. They feasted on the* **feisty** *little squirrels that* **bolted** *from tree to tree and on the flocks of willow grouse that seemed to be everywhere.*

With the warm days of spring came the time for muskrat hunting. The women long ago **had been tutored in** *the skills and patience required. First, special nets and traps had to be made. A willow branch was bent into a circle and bound securely at the ends. The women wove thin strips of moose leather into the frames until each formed* **a crude but sturdy** *net. Then, on a*

....

feisty lively
bolted jumped
had been tutored in were taught
a crude but sturdy an ugly but strong

sunny day, they set out in search of a muskrat tunnel.

They walked a long way before they came to a cluster of lakes **with signs of muskrat life**. They picked out a lake with little black lumps of muskrat houses still showing on the rotting ice. After locating the muskrat tunnel, the women marked each end of the underground pathway with a stick. When the stick moved, it meant a muskrat was coming through the tunnel and when it emerged from the opening, one of the women would **snatch it with her net and end its life** with a blow to the head. The first day, the women caught ten muskrats. But they were worn out by the stress of bending down and waiting, so the walk back to camp seemed long.

The spring days brought little time to talk or to reflect on the past as the women kept busy catching more muskrats and some beavers, all of which were smoke-dried

....

with signs of muskrat life where they thought muskrats lived

snatch it with her net and end its life quickly take it and kill it

for preservation. Their days were so full they hardly took time to eat, and at night they slept deeply. When they decided they had caught more than their share of muskrat and beaver, they packed everything and hauled it back to their main camp.

Still, the women felt vulnerable. The area was rich in animal life now, and they felt in time other people might come. Normally, other people **meant their own kind**. But since being left behind on that cold winter day, the women felt **defenseless against** the younger generation and had lost trust that they knew they never could regain. Now, **suspicion left them wary of** what might happen if anyone were to come upon them and find their growing store of food. They talked about what they should do, and in time they agreed they should move to a place less desirable—a place other people would not wish to explore, perhaps a place where it would be hard to **manage the mighty swarms** of summer insects.

The women did not relish having to face the many blood-thirsty mosquitoes that awaited them in the thick willow bushes and trees. But their fear of people was greater. So they packed all they had and began the unpleasant trek to the hiding place. They decided to work in the heat of the day when mosquitoes seemed to hide. At night, they sat near a smoky fire to protect themselves. It took days to transfer the camp, but at last, the women stood

....

meant their own kind were members of their band
defenseless against that they were not safe from
suspicion left them wary of they worried about
manage the mighthy swarms handle the big groups

by the creek and took one last look around, wishing a wind would blow away any hints of their presence.

Before deciding to move, the women had torn large amounts of birch bark from the trees. Now they recognized their mistake. Although by habit they took pieces of bark from trees spaced far apart, the women knew that **any alert eye would take notice of this detail**. But they also knew that nothing could be done about it, and in resignation they left the camp for their less desirable place within the thickets.

The two women spent the remaining days of spring trying to make their new camp more hospitable. They put up their shelters under the deep shade of tall spruce trees and hidden among many willows. Then they found a cool spot where they dug a deep hole that they lined with willows. There, they laid their large cache of dried meat for the summer. They also placed a few traps atop the ground to scare off any sharp-nosed predators. The mosquitoes were everywhere, and as they worked, the women relied on long-used methods of shielding themselves to keep from **being eaten alive**. They hung leather tassles around their faces and their thick clothing to keep the small insects from biting into their skin. When **it seemed as if they would be carried away**, the women covered their skin with muskrat grease to repel the masses of flying pests. Meanwhile, they charted a small hidden path to the creek

....

any alert eye would take notice of this detail The People would know that someone had used the camp

being eaten alive getting bitten all over

it seemed as if they would be carried away the bugs were attacking them too much

where they got their water and, with summer **nearly upon them**, made their fish traps. Once the traps were set, the women had no trouble catching fish and found they had to move nearer to the creek to keep up with the task of cutting and drying. In time, a bear began helping himself to the fish the women had stored. This worried them, but in time they **reached an unusual agreement** with the bear. They carried the fish guts far from the camp where the greedy bear could **laze about** and eat at his leisure.

Too soon, the sun lay orange and cool on the evening horizon, and the women knew summer was dwindling. About this time, the spawning salmon began to find their way up the little creek, much to the women's pleasure, and for a short while they were busy with the reddish fish meat. The bear disappeared from the area, but still the women disposed of fish innards far down the creek. If the bear did not eat them, the ever-present ravens would devour them soon enough. The women also were **frugal**, and they preserved many inside parts of the fish for other uses. For instance, the salmon intestines could be used for containing water, and the skin was fashioned into round bags to hold dried fish. These tasks kept them so busy they were up from early morning until late at night, and before they knew it, the short Arctic summer passed, and fall crept upon them.

When the season changed, the women retired from

....

nearly upon them coming soon

reached an unusual agreement made a deal

laze about relax

frugal careful about saving everything

fishing and hauled their large supply back to the hidden camp. There they found a new problem. They had collected so much fish that there was no place to store it, and with the approaching winter there was no shortage of small animals searching for winter food. Eventually, the women made standing caches for their fish, and they placed great bundles of thorns and brush beneath them to discourage animals from bothering the fish. Perhaps this method worked, or perhaps it was just their luck, but animals kept away from their caches.

Far behind the camp was a low hill that the women had not had time to explore. One day, with their summer hunting finished, Sa' found herself wondering what **bounties might lie** on that hill or around it. So she took her spear and bow and the arrows the women had made, announcing that she would visit the hill. Ch'idzigyaak did not approve but could see that her friend **would not be deterred**.

"Just keep the fire going, and your spear nearby, and you should be safe," Sa' said as she set out, leaving Ch'idzigyaak behind shaking her head in disapproval.

It was **a day of abandon** for Sa'. She felt light-hearted for the first time in more years than she could remember, and like a child, she **grasped greedily at** the feeling. The day was beautiful. The leaves were turning a brilliant gold and the air was crisp and clear as Sa' all but skipped

....

bounties might lie wonderful things she might find
would not be deterred could not be stopped
a day of abandon a great time of freedom
grasped greedily at enjoyed

along an animal trail. From a distance, one would not be
able to see that Sa' was an older woman, for she looked
lithe and energetic. When she reached the top, she gasped
in surprise. Before her lay vast patches of cranberries.
Sa' dropped to her knees and began to scoop handfuls of
the small red fruit, stuffing them into her mouth. As she
gorged on this delicious food, a movement in the nearby
brush made her freeze instantly.

Slowly, Sa' forced herself to look toward the sound,
imagining the worst. She relaxed when she saw that it was
only a bull moose. Then she remembered that this time of
year a bull moose could be the most **fearful animal on
four legs**. Usually timid, the bull moose in his **rutting
stage** was no longer afraid of man or of anything else that
moved or stood in his way.

The moose remained still for a long time as if he were

....

lithe flexible
gorged on quickly ate
fearful animal on four legs dangerous animal
rutting stage competitive time of year

just as surprised and undecided about the small woman who stood before him as she had been about him. As her pulse slowed almost to normal, Sa' imagined the **delectable** taste of moose meat during the long winter months ahead. In another moment of unthinking craziness, she reached for an arrow from her pack and placed it in her bow. The moose's ears flipped forward at the movement, then it turned and ran in the opposite direction just as the arrow landed harmlessly on the soft ground.

Pressing her fate, Sa' followed. She could not run as strongly as when she was young, but with something that looked more like a limp than a jog, Sa' was able to pursue the large animal. A moose can outrun a human any time unless, of course, there is too much snow. But on a snowless day like this, the moose sprinted far ahead as Sa', gasping for breath, barely caught a glimpse of his large hind-end disappearing behind the brush. The big bull stopped many times, almost as if he were playing a game with Sa', and just when she almost **caught up**, he would saunter far ahead once more. Normally, a moose will run as far as he can from any predator. But today, the moose did not feel much like running, nor did he feel threatened, so the old woman was able to keep him in sight. She was stubborn and would not give up, although she knew that she **was outmatched**. By late afternoon, the moose seemed to grow tired of the game as he watched her from the corner of his dark round

....

delectable delicious
Pressing her fate Putting herself in more danger
caught up was close to the bull
was outmatched could not win

eyes, and with one flip of his ear he began to run faster. Only then did Sa' admit to herself that there was no way she could catch it. She stared at the empty brush in defeat. Slowly she turned back, thinking to herself, "If only I were forty years younger, I might have caught him."

It was late that night when Sa' returned to the camp where her friend kept watch by a large campfire. As Sa' sank wearily into a bundle of spruce boughs, Ch'idzigyaak could not help but blurt out, "**I think many more years were taken from me while I worried for you.**" Despite the **admonishment** in her voice, Ch'idzigyaak was deeply relieved that no harm had come to her friend.

Knowing that she had been foolish, Sa' understood what her friend had been through and she felt ashamed. Ch'idzigyaak handed her a bowl of warm fish meat and Sa' ate slowly. When a little of her strength returned, Sa' told Ch'idzigyaak how she spent the day. Ch'idzigyaak smiled as she envisioned her friend chasing the long-legged bull, but she did not smile too broadly for **it was not in her nature** to laugh at others. Sa' was grateful for that, and then, remembering the cranberries, told her friend about the great find and they both were cheered.

It took a few days for Sa' to recover from her adventure with the moose, so the two old women sat still and wove birch bark into large round bowls. Then they went back to the hill and gathered as many berries as they could

....

I think many more years were taken from me while I worried for you I was worried about your safety

admonishment sadness and anger

it was not in her nature she believed it was not kind

carry. By that time, autumn was upon them and the nights became chillier, reminding the women that there was no time to waste in gathering their winter wood supply.

They piled wood high around their cache and shelter, and when they cleared all the wood from the area around the camp, they walked far back into the forest, packing in more bundles of wood on their backs. This went on until snowflakes fell from the sky, and one day the women awoke to a land shrouded in white. Now that winter was near, the women spent more time inside their shelter by the warm fire. Their days seemed easier now that they were prepared.

Soon the women **fell into a daily routine of** collecting wood, checking rabbit snares, and melting snow for water. They sat evenings by the campfire, keeping each other company. During the months past, the women were too busy to think about what had happened to them, and if the thought **did cross their minds,** they blocked it out. But now that they had nothing else to do in the evenings, those unwelcome thoughts kept coming back until soon each woman began to talk less as each stared thoughtfully into the small fire. They felt it was a taboo to think of those who had abandoned them, but now **the treacherous thoughts invaded their minds**.

The darkness grew longer, and the land became silent and still. It took much concentration for the two women

....

fell into a daily routine of spent each day

did cross their minds came to them

the treacherous thoughts invaded their minds they could not stop thinking about those painful memories

to fill their long days with work. They made many **articles** of rabbit-fur clothing such as mittens, hats, and face coverings. Yet, **despite this**, they felt a great loneliness slowly **enclose** them.

....

articles kinds, pieces
despite this no matter what they did
enclose surround, fill

BEFORE YOU MOVE ON...

1. Predict Reread page 71. The women make a mistake taking bark from the trees. What could happen?

2. Character Ch'idzigyaak worries when Sa' is gone. What does this show about her?

LOOK AHEAD Read pages 79–87 to see how the chief feels about having left the old women behind.

CHAPTER 6
Sadness among The People

The chief stood **surveying** his surroundings with eyes made a little older by deep sadness. His people were in a desperate state, their **eyes and cheeks sunk low in gaunt faces** and their tattered clothing barely able to keep out the freezing cold. Many of them were frostbitten. **Luck had gone against them.** In desperation, still searching for game, they had returned to the place where they abandoned the two old women the winter before.

Sadly, the chief remembered how he fought the urge to turn back and save the old ones. But taking them back into the band would have been the worst thing for him to

....

surveying looking over
eyes and cheeks sunk low in gaunt faces faces thin from not eating
Luck had gone against them. Things were going badly.

do. Many of the more ambitious younger men would have seen this as an act of weakness. And the way things had been going, The People would have been easily convinced that their leader was not dependable. No, the chief had known that a drastic change in leadership would have proved more damaging than the hunger, for in times when a band is starving, **bad politics lead only to further disaster**. The chief remembered that moment of terrible weakness when he had almost allowed his emotions to ruin them all.

Now, once more, The People were suffering, and this winter found them on the verge of hopelessness. After **turning their backs on** the old women, The People traveled many hard miles before coming on a small herd of caribou. The meat sustained them until spring when they began to harvest fish, ducks, muskrats, and beaver. But just when they regained their energy to hunt and dry their food, the summer season ended, and it was time to think of moving toward the place where they would be able to find winter meat. The chief had never known such terrible luck. As they traveled, the fall season came and went, and once more the band found itself nearly out of food. Now the chief looked at The People wearily with a feeling of panic and self-doubt. How long could he hold out before he, too, became **lost in the hunger and fatigue that undermined his decisions**? The People seemed to have given up trying to survive. They no longer cared to hear his lectures, staring at

....

bad politics lead only to further disaster the chief must appear strong for his people

turning their backs on abandoning

lost in the hunger and fatigue that undermined his decisions too hungry and tired to think clearly

him with dulled eyes as if he made no sense.

Something else that troubled the chief was his decision to return to the place where they had left the old women. No one argued as he led them here, but the chief knew they were surprised. Now they stood looking around as if they expected something from him, or expected to see the two women. The chief avoided their eyes, not wanting them to know that he was as confused as they were. There was not a single sign that anyone had been left here. Not one bone **gave evidence** that the old ones had died. Even if an animal had **stripped their bones of flesh**, surely something would have been left behind to show that humans had died here. But there was nothing, not even the tent that had sheltered the women.

Among The People was a guide named Daagoo. He was an old man, younger than the two old women, but still considered an elder. In his younger days, Daagoo had been **a tracker**, but **the years had dimmed** his vision and skills. He observed out loud what none of the others would acknowledge. "Maybe they moved on," he said in a low voice so that only the chief would hear him. But in the silence, many heard him and some felt a surge of hope for the women many had loved.

After setting up camp, the chief summoned the guide and three of his strongest young hunters. "I do not know what is going on, but I have a feeling that all is not as it

....

gave evidence could be found to prove
stripped their bones of flesh eaten the women
a tracker an expert in the band at following trails
the years had dimmed old age lessened

appears to be. I want you to go to the camps near here and see what you can find."

The chief was quiet about what he suspected, but he knew that the guide and the three hunters would understand, especially Daagoo, for he had watched the chief from season to season and had come to know what the man was thinking. Daagoo respected the chief and realized that he **suffered from self-loathing** because of the part he had played in abandoning the old women. The guide knew the chief despised his own weakness, for it showed in the **hard lines of bitterness etched** on his face. The old man sighed. He knew that soon the self-hate would take its toll, and he did not like the thought of a good man such as the chief being destroyed this way. Yes, he would try to find out what had happened to the women, even if the effort was wasted.

Long after the four men left camp the chief stared after them. He could not find a definite reason why he wasted precious energy and time on what might be **a futile** effort. Yet he, too, had a strange feeling of hope. Hope for what? He had no answer. All the chief knew for sure was that in hard times The People should hold together, and last winter they had not done so. They had **inflicted an injustice on** themselves and the two old women, and he knew that The People had suffered silently since that day. It would be good if the two women survived, but the chief knew

....

suffered from self-loathing hated himself
hard lines of bitterness etched sadness expressed
a futile an unsuccessful
inflicted an injustice on hurt

the odds weighed against that hope. How could two feeble ones survive freezing cold without food or the strength to hunt? The chief acknowledged this, yet he could not still the small speck of hope that sprang from months of hardship. Finding the women alive would give The People a second chance and that, perhaps, was what he hoped for most.

Each of the four men was conditioned to run long distances. What took the two women days to travel to the first camp the year before took the four men a single day. They found nothing but endless snow and trees. The trek **taxed their limited energy**, and they decided to spend the night there. When the first hint of morning dawned, the men were up and jogging once more.

Daylight was fading when the men arrived at the second camp, and the younger men saw no evidence that it had been used in a long time. **Impatience began to overtake them.** They had been trained from childhood to respect their elders, but sometimes they thought they knew more than the older ones. Although they did not say so out loud, they felt precious time was being wasted when they should be hunting for moose.

"Let's turn back now," one of the young men suggested, and the others agreed quickly.

The guide's eyes lit up in amusement. How impatient they were! Yet Daagoo did not criticize the others for he, too, had been impatient as a young man. Instead, he

....

the odds weighed against that hope it was not likely they survived

taxed their limited energy tired them completely

Impatience began to overtake them. They thought looking for the women was not a good idea.

said, "Take a closer look around you." The young hunters looked at him impatiently.

"Look closely at those birch trees," Daagoo insisted, and the men stared **blankly** at the trees. They saw nothing unusual. Daagoo sighed, and this caught the attention of one of the younger men, who tried again to see what the old man saw. **Finally, his eyes widened.** "Look!" he said, pointing to an empty patch on a birch tree. Then they saw that other trees spaced widely throughout the area had been stripped carefully, almost as if done **intentionally** so that no one would notice.

"Maybe it was another band," one of the men said.

"Why would they try to hide those empty spots on the trees?" Daagoo asked. The young man shrugged, unable to find an answer.

Then Daagoo gave them instructions. "Before we return," he said, "I want to search this area." Before they could protest, the guide pointed them off in different directions. "If you see anything unusual, come right back here and we will go together to see what it is." Tired as they were, the men began their search, although they were sulky and did not believe that the two women still lived.

Meanwhile, Daagoo set out in the direction he believed the two old women might have taken. "If I were afraid to be found by The People who left me to die, I would go this way," he muttered to himself. "It is **a senseless** direction

....

blankly unknowingly

Finally, his eyes widened. He saw what Daagoo saw.

intentionally purposely; with great thought

a senseless an unusual

because it is far from water. But in winter they would not have to rely on the river, so I think they might be this way."

Daagoo walked a long distance into the willows and beneath the tall spruce trees. As he trudged farther and farther over the snow, he felt weary and wondered if he was doing the right thing. How was it possible to believe that two old women could survive when they, The People, **barely made it through** that winter? Especially those two women. All they did was complain. Even when little children were hungry, the women complained and criticized. Many times, Daagoo expected someone to silence them, but that had not happened until the day **things had gotten out of control**. Daagoo began to feel they were on a useless hunt. The two women must have gotten lost and died along the way. Perhaps they had tried to cross the river and drowned.

As Daagoo thought about all of this, he became more doubtful with each negative thought. Then, suddenly, he smelled something. In the crystal-clear winter air, a light scent of smoke drifted past his nose and was gone. Daagoo stood very still as he tried to **catch the scent** once more, but there was nothing. For a moment, he wondered if it had been his imagination. Perhaps a summer fire nearby had left its lingering smell in the air. Not wanting to believe that, the old man backtracked slowly until once

....

barely made it through almost did not survive

things had gotten out of control they abandoned the women

catch the scent find the smell

again he caught the scent. It was a light smell, but this time Daagoo knew that it was no remnant of a summer fire. No, this smoke had a freshness about it. Excited, he tried walking first in one direction, then another until the smoke grew stronger. Convinced that it came from a campfire nearby, **his face crinkled into a broad grin as a certainty filled him**—the two women had survived.

Daagoo hurried back to get the young men who were waiting as impatiently as before. They did not want to follow when he **beckoned, but reluctantly**, they followed Daagoo into the night for what seemed a long time. Finally, the guide held out his hand signaling them to stop. Lifting his nose, he told them to smell the air. The hunters sniffed but did not smell anything. "What is it you want us to smell?" one of them asked.

"Just keep smelling," Daagoo answered, so the men sniffed the air again until one exclaimed, "I smell smoke!" The others walked around sniffing the air with more interest now until they, too, smelled it. Still **skeptical**, one of the younger men asked Daagoo what he expected to find. "We will see," he said simply as he led them farther toward the smoke.

The guide's eyes strained into the darkness looking for the light of a campfire. He saw nothing but outlines of spruce trees and willows. Aided by the small lights of the many stars above, Daagoo saw that the snow was

....

his face crinkled into a broad grin as a certainty filled him he smiled and knew

beckoned, but reluctantly called to them, but slowly

skeptical doubtful

untrampled. Everything was still and quiet. Yet, the evidence of smoke told him that somewhere near someone was camping. As sure as **the blood raced through his veins**, the old tracker was now confident that the two old women were alive and at that moment, close. He could not contain his excitement, turning to the younger men and saying, "The two old women are near." **Chills ran down the spines of the younger men.** They still did not believe that the old ones had survived.

Cupping his hands to his mouth, Daagoo called the women's names into the velvet night and **identified himself.** Then he waited, hearing only the sound of his own words swallowed by the silence.

....

the blood raced through his veins he was alive

Chills ran down the spines of the younger men. The younger men were amazed.

identified himself told them who he was

BEFORE YOU MOVE ON...

1. **Conflict** Reread pages 79–80. The chief feels both confident and confused about leaving the old women. Why?

2. **Sequence** Reread pages 84–87. Describe how Daagoo discovers the trail of the two old women.

LOOK AHEAD Will the strength of the old women last? Read pages 88–98 to find out.

CHAPTER 7
The stillness is broken

C h'idzigyaak and Sa' had settled down for the night. As usual, after doing their daily chores and eating their supper, the two women sat and talked over their fire. They spoke more of The People these days. Loneliness and time had **healed their most bitter** memories, and the hate and fear **born from last year's unexpected betrayal** seemed to **have been numbed by** the many nights they spent sitting and listening to their own thoughts. It all seemed like a distant dream. Now, with their bellies full, the women found themselves in the comfort of their shelter speaking of how much they

....

healed their most bitter *made them feel better about their worst*

born from last year's unexpected betrayal *that began when their band left them behind*

have been numbed by *go away with*

missed The People. When they ran out of conversation, the women sat silently, each **wrapped in** her own thoughts.

Suddenly, out of the stillness, the women heard their names called. From across the campfire, **their eyes met**, and they knew what they heard was not their imagination. The man's voice became loud, and he identified himself. The women knew the old guide. Perhaps they could trust him. But what of the others? It was Ch'idzigyaak who spoke first. "Even if we do not answer, they will find us."

Sa' agreed. "Yes, they will find us," she said as her mind raced with many thoughts.

"What will we do?" Ch'idzigyaak whined in panic.

Sa' took a while to think. Then she said, "We must let them know we are here." Seeing the look of **hysteria** enter her friend's eyes, Sa' hastened to say in smooth, confident tones, "We must be brave and face them. But my friend, be prepared for anything." She waited a moment before she added, "Even death." This did not comfort Ch'idzigyaak, who looked as frightened as her friend ever had seen her.

The two women sat a long time trying to gather what courage they had left. They knew they could run no longer. Finally, Sa' got up slowly and went outside into the cold night air, **hollering rather hoarsely**, "We are here!"

Daagoo had been standing patiently, alertly, while the young hunters eyed him in doubt. What if it were someone else? An enemy perhaps? Just as one of the men was about

....

wrapped in focused on
their eyes met they looked at each other
hysteria panic, fear
hollering rather hoarsely yelling in a rough voice

to voice doubts, out of the darkness they heard Sa' answer. The old guide's face broke into a wide smile. He knew it! They were alive. Immediately, they headed in the direction of the sound. The cold air made the woman's voice seem close, but it took the men some time to reach the camp.

Finally, the men approached the light of the campfire that had been built outside the shelter. Standing by it were the two old women armed with long, sharp, dangerous-looking spears. Daagoo had to smile in admiration of the old women who stood like two warriors ready to defend themselves. "We **mean you no harm**," he assured them.

The women stared at him **defiantly** a moment before Sa' said, "I believe you come **in peace**. But why are you here?" The guide stood a moment, unsure how to explain **himself**. "The chief sent me here to find you. He believed you were alive and told us to find you."

"Why?" Ch'idzigyaak asked suspiciously.

"I do not know," Daagoo said simply. Indeed, he was surprised to find that he did not know what he or the chief thought would happen once they found the two women, for it was obvious that the women did not trust him or the other men. "I will have to return to the chief to report that we have found you," he said. The two women knew this. "What then?" Sa' asked.

The guide shrugged. "I do not know. But the chief will protect you no matter what happens."

....

mean you no harm are not here to hurt you
defiantly angrily
in peace as friends
himself why they had come

"Like he did the last time?" Ch'idzigyaak asked sharply.

Daagoo knew that if he wanted to, he and the three hunters easily could **overtake** these two women and their weapons. Yet, he felt his admiration grow stronger because the two women were ready to fight whatever they had to face. These were not the same women he had known before.

"**You have my word**," he said quietly, and the women could **feel the magnitude** of what he said as they stood still a long time.

Sa' noticed how worn and weary the men looked. Even the guide who stood proudly **had a destitute look about him**. "You look tired," she said in a grudging tone. "Come inside," and she led them into their spacious and warm shelter.

....

overtake attack and win against
You have my word I promise you
feel the magnitude understand the importance
had a destitute look about him looked very weak

The four men entered the tent cautiously, knowing that they were not welcome guests. The women motioned them to sit down, and after the men were seated around the warm fire, Sa' dug around in the back of her bedding along the tent wall and pulled out a fishbag, handing a portion of dried fish to each of the men. As the men ate the fish, they looked around. They could see that the women's bedding was made of newly-woven rabbit fur. The two women looked to be in better shape than The People. How could that be? After the men ate their dried fish, Sa' served them boiled rabbit broth, which they drank gratefully.

Meanwhile, Ch'idzigyaak sat to the side staring **rather balefully** at the hunters, making them feel uncomfortable. With astonishment, the men realized these two women not only had survived but also sat before them in good health while they, the strongest men of the band, were half-starved.

Sa' also stared at the men as they ate their food. She noticed that they tried to eat slowly, but now that they were in the light, she could tell from their lean faces that they had not been eating well. Ch'idzigyaak noticed this, too, but **her heart was filled with resentment at this unwanted intrusion**, and she did not feel pity. When the men finished their food, Daagoo looked at the women expectantly as he waited for them to say something.

For a while no one **broke the silence**. Finally, Daagoo

....

rather balefully angrily

her heart was filled with resentment at this unwanted intrusion she was still mad and did not want the men to come in their tent

broke the silence spoke

said, "The chief believed that you survived, so he sent us to find you." Ch'idzigyaak let out an angry grunt, and when the men turned to her, she gave them a mean look and turned her face away. She could not believe that these people **had the nerve** to search for them. Surely Sa' could see that they **were up to no good**. Sa' reached out and patted her friend's hand **consolingly**, then turned to the men and said simply, "Yes, we have survived."

Daagoo's mouth twitched in amusement at Ch'idzigyaak's wrath. Yet Sa' seemed **not to hold too much of a grudge**, so he avoided the glaring eyes of Ch'idzigyaak and spoke to Sa' instead. "We are starving, and the cold gets worse. Again we have little food, and we are in the same shape as when we left you. But when the chief hears you are well, he will ask you to come back to our group. The chief and most of The People feel as I do. We are sorry for what was done to you."

The women sat silently a long time. Finally Sa' said, "So you may leave us alone once more just when we need you the most?" Daagoo took a few minutes to respond, wishing the chief was there to answer, for the chief was more experienced in answering such questions.

"I cannot say that it will not happen again. In hard times, some grow meaner than wolves, and others grow scared and weak, like I did when you were left behind." Daagoo's voice filled with sudden emotion at those last

---

had the nerve were rude enough
were up to no good could not be trusted
consolingly softly to comfort her
not to hold too much of a grudge less angry

words, but he steadied his voice and continued. "I can tell you one thing right now. If it ever does happen again, I will **protect you with my own life** as long as I live." As he spoke, Daagoo realized that in these two women, whom he once thought of as helpless and weak, he had rediscovered the inner strength that **had deserted him** the winter before. Now, somehow, he knew that he never would believe himself to be old and weak again. Never!

The younger men had sat quietly and listened to the exchange between their elders. Now, one of them spoke out in a youthfully passionate voice, "I, too, will protect you if anyone ever tries to do you harm again." Everyone looked at him in surprise. Then **his peers also vowed** to protect the two women, for they had been witness to a miraculous survival and had regained a stronger sense of respect for the old ones. The women could feel their hearts soften at these words. Still, there was distrust, for, though they believed these men, the women were unsure about the others.

The two women huddled together for a private conference. "Can we trust them?" Ch'idzigyaak asked. Sa' paused a moment, then nodded her head and said softly, "Yes."

"What of the other people? What if they knew of our caches? Do you think they will **hold back** when they see all our food? Look how hungry these men are. Last year they did not respect us. Here you are willing to let them

....

protect you with my own life fight for your safety
had deserted him he had lost
his peers also vowed the others also promised
hold back stop themselves from robbing us

come to us! My friend, I fear that they will take our food from us whether we like it or not," Ch'idzigyaak said. Sa' already had thought of this, but she was not afraid. Instead, she answered, "We have to remember that they are suffering. Yes, they were too quick to **condemn us**, but now we have proven them wrong. If they **do the same thing**, we both know that we can survive. We have proven that much to ourselves. Now we must **put aside our pride** long enough to remember that they are suffering. If not for the adults, then for the children. Could you forget your own grandson?"

Ch'idzigyaak knew her friend was right, as usual. No, she could not be so selfish as to let her grandson go hungry when she had so much food to eat. The men waited patiently as the two women whispered between themselves.

Sa' was not through talking, for she knew that Ch'idzigyaak still harbored fear about what was happening and needed confidence to face the future. "They do not know we have done well for ourselves," she said. "But tomorrow in the daylight they will see, and then we will know if what they say is true. But remember this, my friend. If they do the same to us again, we will survive. And if they truly mean what they say, then maybe we will always **be a reminder to them** in harder times ahead."

Ch'idzigyaak nodded in agreement. For a moment, seeing these members of the band, she felt her old fears

....

condemn us make their decision to leave us behind
do the same thing leave us behind again
put aside our pride control our anger
be a reminder to them remind them of our strength

and forgot **her renewed strength**. She looked at her friend with great fondness. Sa' always seemed to know the right thing to say.

In the shelter that night, the two women and the guide exchanged stories while the younger men sat in respectful and attentive silence. The old man told all that had happened after The People left the two women behind. He spoke of the ones who had died. Most were children. Unshed tears glistened in the old women's eyes as they listened, for they had loved some of these people, and the children were among their favorites. The women could not bear to think of how much the children might have suffered before they died so young and so cruelly.

After Daagoo finished his story, Sa' told him how they survived. The men sat with mixed emotions. The story she told sounded unbelievable, yet **the women's very presence was evidence of its truth**. Sa' did not mind the look of awe she saw in the men's faces. She continued telling her story as she **looked back into** the eventful year she and Ch'idzigyaak had shared. When she ended her story by telling them of their many food caches, their visitors' eyes became alert.

"When we heard your voice the first time, we knew we could trust you. We also knew that since you were able to find us in the night that it would take little time for you to find our food caches, too. That is why I am telling

....

her renewed strength how strong she had become

the women's very presence was evidence of its truth the fact that the women survived proved the story was true

looked back into remembered

you now. We know you mean us no harm." Sa' spoke directly to Daagoo. "But what of The People? If they can do such a thing as leave us behind, then they will have no feelings about taking what is ours. They will think of us again as weak and old with no need for our large caches. I do not blame them now for what they have done to us, for my friend and I know what hunger can do to a person. But we have worked hard for what we have, and though we knew it would be too much for us to eat during the winter, we stored it anyway. Maybe it was because we thought **this might happen**." Sa' paused to consider her words carefully. Then she added, "We will share with The People, but they must not become greedy and try to take our food, for we will fight to our deaths for what is ours."

The men sat in silence listening to Sa' speak in a strong and passionate voice. Then she **laid down their terms**: "You will stay at the old camp. We do not wish to see anyone else but you," Sa' motioned to Daagoo, "and the chief. We will give you food, and we hope The People will eat **sparingly in knowledge of** harder times to come. This is all we can do for you." The guide nodded in acknowledgement and said in a quiet voice, "I will return with this message to the chief."

After they said all that had to be said, the women invited the men to sleep on one side of the shelter. For the first time in a long time, the women felt themselves relax.

....

this might happen the band might return to us

laid down their terms told them what the women wanted the band to do

sparingly in knowledge of very little so that we will have food for the

In those long months they feared many things. Now their visions of wolves and other predators faded away, and the women **fell into a worry-free sleep**.

They were no longer alone.

....

fell into a worry-free sleep went to sleep without any worries

BEFORE YOU MOVE ON...

1. **Comparisons** Reread page 92. How does the condition of the old women differ from that of the strongest men?

2. **Plot** Reread page 97. What plans does Sa' make to protect herself and Ch'idzigyaak?

LOOK AHEAD Read pages 99–108 to see if the group accepts the old women again.

CHAPTER 8
A new beginning

Before the men left the next day, the women packed large bundles of dry fish, enough to **restore The People's energy for travel**. Meanwhile, the chief waited anxiously. He feared that something had happened to his men, yet **hope kept intruding on that thought**. When the men returned, the chief quickly gathered the **council** to hear their story.

The guide told the stunned people what they had discovered. When he finished his story, he told them that the women did not trust them and did not want to see them. Daagoo told them of the terms the women had set.

....

restore The People's energy for travel give The People
strength to move to the new camp
hope kept intruding on that thought he felt hopeful
council respected members of the band

After a few minutes of silence, the chief said, "We will **respect the women's wishes**. Anyone who disagrees will have to fight me."

Daagoo was quick to join in, "The young men and I will stand by you." The council members who had suggested abandoning the two old women were deeply ashamed. Finally, one of them spoke. "We were wrong to leave them behind. They proved it so. Now we will pay them back with respect."

After the chief announced the news to all, The People agreed to follow the rules set by the two women. After their energy was restored by the nourishing dried fish, The People began to pack, for they could not wait to see the two women. In this time of hardship the news of their survival filled the band with a sense of hope and awe. Ch'idzigyaak's daughter, Ozhii Nelii, wept when she heard the news. She had believed her mother to be dead but knew, **despite her own overwhelming relief**, that her mother would never forgive her. Shruh Zhuu was so ecstatic that, when he heard the news, the young boy immediately gathered his things and was ready to go.

It took the band quite a while to reach the camp where the bark had been stripped off the birch trees. The chief and Daagoo had gone ahead to meet with the two women, and when they arrived at the women's camp, the chief had to **contain himself from embracing** them. The women

....

respect the women's wishes do as they ask

despite her own overwhelming relief even though she was relieved

contain himself from embracing stop himself from hugging

eyed him with distrust, so they all sat down to talk instead. The women told the chief what they expected from The People. He responded by telling them their wishes would be obeyed. "We will give you enough food for The People, and when it becomes low, we will give you more food. We will give you small portions at a time," Sa' told the chief, who nodded his head almost humbly.

It took another day before the band reached the new camp, unpacked and set up tents. Then the chief and his men arrived with bundles of fish and rabbit-fur clothing. Daagoo had hinted boldly to the old women of the poor condition of the band's clothing after he spotted their large collection of rabbit-fur garments. The women both knew they never would use the many mittens, head coverings, blankets and vests they had made in their spare time, so they felt obligated to share with those who needed them. After The People settled down in their new camp and **their bellies no longer cried for nourishment**, they became more curious about the two old women. But they were forbidden to go near that camp.

The colder days came and stayed a long time, and The People carefully rationed the food that the old women shared. Then the hunters killed a large moose and hauled it many miles back to the camp where **all rejoiced at the good fortune**.

All this time the chief and the guide took turns making

....

eyed looked at

their bellies no longer cried for nourishment they no longer felt hungry

all rejoiced at the good fortune everyone was happy about their good luck

daily visits to the women. When it became apparent that the two women also were curious about The People, the chief asked permission for others to visit, too. Ch'idzigyaak was quick to say no, for her pride was the strongest. But later, the two women talked about it and admitted to themselves that they were ready for visitors. This was especially **so** for Ch'idzigyaak, who missed her family terribly. When the chief arrived the next day, the two women told him of their decision, and soon people began visiting. At first they were timid and unsure. But after a few visits, they all talked more easily, and soon laughter and light-hearted chatter could be heard from inside the shelter. Each time the visitors came, they brought the two women gifts of moosemeat or animal furs, which the women accepted gratefully.

Relations became better between The People and the two women. Both learned that **from hardship, a side of people emerged that they had not known**. The People had thought themselves to be strong, yet they had been weak. And the two old ones whom they thought to be the most helpless and useless had proven themselves to be strong. Now, an unspoken understanding existed between them, and The People found themselves **seeking out the company of** the two women for advice and to learn new things. Now they realized that because the two women had lived so long, surely they knew a lot more than

....

so true

from hardship, a side of people emerged that they had not known people can do surprising things when times are difficult

seeking out the company of wanting to speak with

J.L. Grant

The People had believed.

Visitors came and went daily from the women's camp. Long after they left, Ch'idzigyaak would stand and stare **after them**. Sa' watched her and felt pity for her friend, for she knew that Ch'idzigyaak expected to see her daughter and grandson, but they did not come. Ch'idzigyaak harbored a secret fear in her heart that perhaps something bad had happened to them and The People did not want to tell her, but she was afraid to ask.

One day, as Ch'idzigyaak gathered wood, a young voice behind her said softly, "I have come for my hatchet." Ch'idzigyaak stood slowly and the wood in her arms fell **unnoticed** to the ground as she turned. They stared at each other, almost **as if they were in a dream and could not believe what they saw**. Faces wet with tears,

....

after them in the direction they went

unnoticed carelessly

as if they were in a dream and could not believe what they saw in disbelief

Ch'idzigyaak and her grandson stared at each other in happiness, and no words seemed worth speaking at that moment. Without further hesitation, Ch'idzigyaak reached out to embrace this young boy whom she loved.

Sa' stood by smiling at the happy reunion. The young boy looked up to see Sa' and went over to her and gave her a gentle hug. Sa' felt her heart swell with love and pride for this youngster.

Still, Ch'idzigyaak wondered about her daughter. Despite all that had happened, Ch'idzigyaak yearned to see her own flesh and blood. **Being the observant one**, Sa' knew this was why her friend seemed sad despite their good fortune. One day after another of the grandson's visits, Sa' reached over and grasped her friend's hand. "She will come," she said simply, and Ch'idzigyaak nodded her head, although she did not quite believe it.

Winter was almost over. **A well-trodden path lay** between the two camps. The People could not get enough of the women's company, especially the children, who spent many hours laughing and playing in the camp while the old women sat beside their shelter and watched. They were grateful to have survived to witness this. **No longer did they take each day for granted.**

The young grandson came every day. He helped his grandmothers with their daily chores as before and listened to their stories. One day, the older woman could wait no

....

Being the observant one Knowing her friend well

A well-trodden path lay Many people came and went freely

No longer did they take each day for granted. The women learned to value each day of their lives.

longer and finally found the courage to ask, "Where is my daughter? Why does she not come?" The young boy answered honestly. "She is in shame, grandmother. She thinks that you have hated her since that day when she turned her back on you. She has cried every day since we parted," the young boy said as he put his arms around her. "I am worried about her, for **she is making herself old with grief**."

Ch'idzigyaak sat listening, and **her heart went out to** her daughter. Yes, she had been very angry. What mother would not be? For all those years she trained her daughter to be strong, only to find **the training had been for nothing**. Yet, Ch'idzigyaak thought to herself, she is not to be blamed for everything. After all, everyone had participated, and her daughter had acted out of fear. She had been frightened for her son's and mother's lives. It was as simple as that. Ch'idzigyaak also acknowledged that her daughter had been brave to leave the bundle of babiche with the two women. To have left a thing of such value with old ones thought to be near death would have been seen as a foolhardy waste.

Yes, she could forgive her daughter. She could even thank her, for she decided that had it not been for the babiche, they might not have survived. Ch'idzigyaak broke out of her thoughts as she realized that her grandson waited for her to say something. Putting her arms around his

....

she is making herself old with grief she is worrying too much

her heart went out to she felt sorry for

the training had been for nothing that her daughter did not defend her shoulders she patted him gently and said, "Tell my daughter that I do not hate her, grandson." Relief **flooded** the boy's face, for he had spent months worrying about his mother and grandmother. Now, everything was almost the way it once was. Without further encouragement, the boy gave his grandmother **an exuberant** hug before he bolted out of the shelter and ran all the way home.

He arrived at the camp breathless. Bursting in on his mother, the excited youth said in between gasps, "Mother! Grandmother wishes to see you! She told me **there are no hard feelings**!" Ozhii Nelii was stunned. She had not expected this, and for a moment her legs became so weak that she had to sit down. Her body trembled, and she looked once more at her son. "Is this true?" she asked. "Yes," Shruh Zhuu replied, and his mother saw that he spoke the truth.

At first, she was afraid to go, for she still felt guilty. But at her son's **gentle insistence**, Ozhii Nelii gathered enough courage to take the long walk to her mother's camp with her son at her side. When they arrived, the two old women were standing outside the shelter, talking. Sa' saw the visitors first, then Ch'idzigyaak turned to see what caused Sa's silence. When she saw her daughter, her mouth opened but words would not come out. Instead, the women stared at each other until Ch'idzigyaak walked to Ozhii Nelii and embraced her tightly, weeping. All that had stood

....

flooded showed on
an exuberant a strong and excited
there are no hard feelings she is not angry with you
gentle insistence polite request that she go

between them **seemed to vanish with the touch**.

Sa' stood with her arms around Shruh Zhuu, tearfully watching mother and daughter find the love they thought was lost forever. Then Ch'idzigyaak turned and walked into the tent, returning with a small bundle that she pressed into her daughter's hands. Ozhii Nelii saw that it was babiche. She did not understand until Ch'idzigyaak leaned forward and whispered something into her daughter's ear. Ozhii Nelii looked surprised a moment, then she, too, smiled. Again the women fell into one another's arms and embraced.

After everyone had been **reunited**, the chief **appointed the two women to honorary positions** within the band. At first, people wanted to help the old ones in any way they could, but the women would not allow too much assistance, for they enjoyed their newly-found

....

seemed to vanish with the touch went away when they hugged

reunited brought together again

appointed the two women to honorary positions gave the women respected titles

independence. So The People showed their respect for the two women by listening to what they had to say.

More hard times were to follow, for in the cold land of the North **it could be no other way**, but The People kept their promise. They never again abandoned any elder. They had learned a lesson taught by two whom they came to love and care for until each died a truly happy old woman.

....

independence ability to do things for themselves

it could be no other way hard times always came

BEFORE YOU MOVE ON...

1. **Summarize** Reread pages 99–100. How does the group respond to the terms set by the two old women?

2. **Mood** How does the mood of the story change once Ch'idzigyaak forgives her daughter?